"A thoughtful and energetic leader, Mark Batterson presses us to consider how we live out our faith in the world around us. When Mark has something to say, I am quick to listen."

FRANK WRIGHT, PhD
PRESIDENT AND CEO, NATIONAL RELIGIOUS BROADCASTERS

"Mark Batterson is one of the outstanding younger leaders in the U.S. today. As a pastor, he demonstrates his gifts and character in leadership and preaching. As a writer, he communicates wisdom and hope with both energy and clarity."

BRIAN MCLAREN
AUTHOR AND ACTIVIST

"As a leader and teacher, Mark Batterson brings imagination, energy, and insight. Mark's genuine warmth and sincerity spill over into his communication, combining an intense love for his community with a passionate desire to see them living the life God dreams for them. I appreciate his willingness to take bold risks and go to extraordinary lengths to reach our culture with a message that is truly relevant."

ED YOUNG
SENIOR PASTOR, FELLOWSHIP CHURCH

"Mark Batterson is one of the church's most forward thinkers. In this book, he compels us to look both behind and ahead to discover answers to the 'whys' in our lives. *In a Pit with a Lion on a Snowy Day* helps us make sense of this beautiful mess we call life."

LINDY LOWRY
EDITOR, *OUTREACH* MAGAZINE

"Mark Batterson is down-to-earth and humble—yet constantly pushes me to grow. I follow him as a leader, admire him as an innovator, and love him as a friend. Mark has become one of the most important voices for a new generation. Anything he touches changes lives. Read this book and you'll see what I mean."

CRAIG GROESCHEL
PASTOR OF LIFECHURCH.TV, AUTHOR OF *CHAZOWN* AND
CONFESSIONS OF A PASTOR

"Mark's passion for God and our generation is contagious. His writing is honest and insightful. Go ahead—chase the lion!"

MARGARET FEINBERG
AUTHOR OF *WHAT THE HECK AM I GOING TO DO WITH MY LIFE?*

IN A PIT WITH A LION ON A SNOWY DAY

MARK BATTERSON

Multnomah Books

IN A PIT WITH A LION ON A SNOWY DAY
published by Multnomah Books

© 2006 by Mark Batterson
International Standard Book Number: 978-1-59052-715-3

Published in association with Eames Literary Services, Nashville, TN

Unless otherwise indicated, Scripture quotations are from:
The Holy Bible, New International Version © 1973, 1984 by International Bible Society,
used by permission of Zondervan Publishing House
Other Scripture quotations are from:
Holy Bible, New Living Translation (NLT) © 1996. Used by permission of
Tyndale House Publishers, Inc. All rights reserved.
The Holy Bible, New King James Version (NKJV) © 1984 by Thomas Nelson, Inc.
The Holy Bible, King James Version (KJV)

Published in the United States by WaterBrook Multnomah, an imprint of the Crown Publishing
Group, a division of Random House Inc., New York.

MULTNOMAH and its mountain colophon are registered trademarks of Random House Inc.

Printed in the United States of America

For information:
Multnomah Books • 12265 Oracle Boulevard, Suite 200 • Colorado Springs, CO 80921

Library of Congress Cataloging-in-Publication Data
Batterson, Mark.
   In a pit with a lion on a snowy day / Mark Batterson.
      p. cm.
   ISBN 1-59052-715-1
   1. Bible. O.T. Samuel, 2nd, XXIII, 20-22—Criticism, interpretation, etc.
   2. Benaiah (Biblical character) I. Title.
BS1325.52.B38 2006
222'.4406—dc22

                                        2006023650

                      09 10—10 9 8 7

Dedicated to Parker, Summer, and Josiah.
May you grow up to become lion chasers.

CONTENTS

Chapter 1: Locking Eyes with Your Lion 9

Chapter 2: The Odd Thing About Odds 21

Chapter 3: Unlearning Your Fears 41

Chapter 4: The Art of Reframing 59

Chapter 5: Guaranteed Uncertainty. 79

Chapter 6: Playing It Safe Is Risky 101

Chapter 7: Grab Opportunity by the Mane 125

Chapter 8: The Importance of Looking Foolish 147

Chapter 9: Unleash the Lion Chaser Within 167

Acknowledgments. 173

Endnotes 175

CHAPTER 1

Locking Eyes with Your Lion

You are responsible forever for
what you have tamed.
ANTOINE DE SAINT-EXUPÉRY

There is an obscure passage in Scripture that I doubt any Sunday school teacher has ever assigned as a memory verse. It wasn't exegeted in any of the systematic theology classes I took in seminary. It has absolutely no bearing on any major biblical doctrines. You may have read it a few times in a one-year Bible, but it probably didn't even make a blip on your radar screen.

Buried in the Old Testament book of 2 Samuel, the twenty-third chapter, the twentieth and twenty-first verses, is one of the most inconceivable and inspirational passages in Scripture:

There was also Benaiah son of Jehoiada, a valiant warrior from Kabzeel. He did many heroic deeds, which included killing two of Moab's mightiest warriors. Another time he chased a lion down into a pit. Then, despite the snow and slippery ground, he caught the lion and killed it. Another time, armed only with a club, he killed a great Egyptian warrior who was armed with a spear. Benaiah wrenched the spear from the Egyptian's hand and killed him with it.

It's easy to read verses like this in the comfortable confines of your home or office and totally miss the monumental acts of courage displayed by Benaiah. Have you ever met anyone or heard of anyone chasing a lion? Sure, Barnum & Bailey have lion tamers. But lion chasers? Benaiah didn't have a hunting rifle or Land Rover. And this was no game-park safari.

Scripture doesn't tell us what Benaiah was doing or where he was going when he encountered this lion. We don't know the time of day or Benaiah's frame of mind. But Scripture does reveal his gut reaction. And it was gutsy. It ranks as one of the most improbable reactions recorded in Scripture. Usually, when the image of a man-eating beast travels through the optical nerve and registers in the visual cortex, the brain has one over-arching message: *Run away.*

Normal people run away from lions. They run as far and as fast as they possibly can. But lion chasers are wired differently.

For the vast majority of us, the only lions we've ever encountered were stuffed or caged. And few of us have experienced hand-to-hand combat that forced us to fight for our lives. But try to put yourself in Benaiah's snow shoes.

Out of the corner of his eye, Benaiah sees something crawling. I don't know how far away the lion is—and their vision is probably obscured by falling snow and frozen breath—but there is a moment when Benaiah and the lion lock eyes. Pupils dilate. Muscles tense. Adrenaline rushes.

What a Hollywood moment.

Imagine watching it on the movie screen with THX surround sound. Your knuckles turn white as you grip the theater seat. Blood pressure escalates. And the entire audience anticipates what will happen next. Lion encounters tend to script the same way. Man runs away like a scaredy-cat. Lion gives chase. And king of the beasts eats manwich for lunch.

But not this time! Almost as improbable as falling up or the second hand on your watch moving counterclockwise, the lion turns tail and Benaiah gives chase.

The camera films the chase at ground level.

Lions can run up to thirty-five miles per hour and leap thirty feet in a single bound. Benaiah doesn't stand a chance, but that doesn't keep him from giving chase. Then the lion makes one critical misstep. The ground gives away beneath his five-hundred-pound frame, and he falls down a steep embankment into a snow-laden pit. For what it's worth, I'm sure the lion landed on his feet. Lions are part of the cat genus, after all.

No one is eating popcorn at this point. Eyes are fixed on the screen. It's the moment of truth as Benaiah approaches the pit.

Almost like walking on thin ice, Benaiah measures every step. He inches up to the edge and peers into the pit. Menacing yellow eyes stare back. The entire audience is thinking the same thing: *Don't even think about it.*

Have you ever had one of those moments where you do something crazy and ask yourself in retrospect: *What was I thinking?* This had to be one of those moments for Benaiah. Who in their right mind chases lions? But Benaiah now has a moment to collect his thoughts, regain his sanity, and get a grip on reality. And the reality is this: *Normal people don't chase lions.*

So Benaiah turns around and walks away. The audience breathes a collective sigh of relief. But Benaiah isn't walking away. He's getting a running start. There is an audible gasp from the audience as Benaiah runs at the pit and takes a flying leap of faith.

The camera pans out.

You see two sets of tracks leading up to the pit's edge. One set of foot prints. One set of paw prints. Benaiah and the lion disappear into the recesses of the pit. The view is obscured to keep it PG-13. And for a few critical moments, the audience is left with just the THX sound track. A deafening roar echoes in the cavernous pit. A bloodcurdling battle cry pierces the soul.

Then dead silence.

Freeze-frame.

Everybody in the theater expects to see a lion shake its mane and strut out of the pit. But after a few agonizing moments of suspense, the shadow of a human form appears as Benaiah climbs out of the pit. The blood from his wounds drips on the freshly fallen snow. Claw marks crisscross his face and spear arm. But Benaiah wins one of the most improbable victories recorded in the pages of Scripture.

A TERRIBLE, HORRIBLE, NO GOOD, VERY BAD DAY

Right at the outset, let me share one of my core convictions: God is in the business of strategically positioning us in the right place at the right time. A sense of destiny is our birthright as followers of Christ. God is awfully good at getting us where He wants us to go. But here's the catch: The right place often seems like the *wrong* place, and the right time often seems like the *wrong* time.

Can I understate the obvious?

Encountering a lion in the wild is typically a bad thing. A really bad thing! Finding yourself in a pit with a lion on a snowy day generally qualifies as a terrible, horrible, no good, very bad day. That combination of circumstances usually spells one thing: *death*.

I don't think anyone would have bet on Benaiah winning this fight—probably not even the riskiest of gamblers. He had to be at least a one-hundred-to-one underdog. And the snowy conditions on game day didn't help his chances.

Scripture doesn't give us a blow-by-blow description of what happened in that pit. All we know is that when the snow settled, the lion was dead and Benaiah was alive. There was one set of paw prints and two sets of footprints.

Now fast-forward two verses and look at what happens in the next scene.

2 Samuel 23:23 says: "And David put [Benaiah] in charge of his bodyguard."

I can't think of too many places I'd rather *not* be than in a pit with a lion on a snowy day. Can you? Getting stuck in a pit with a lion on a snowy day isn't on anybody's *wish list*. It's a *death wish*. But you've got to admit something: "I killed a lion in a pit on a snowy day" looks pretty impressive on your résumé if you're applying for a bodyguard position with the King of Israel!

You know what I'm saying?

I can picture David flipping through a stack of résumés. "I majored in security at the University of Jerusalem." Nope. "I did an internship with the Palace Guard." Nada. "I worked for Brinks Armored Chariots." Thanks but no thanks.

Then David comes to the next résumé in the stack. "I killed a lion in a pit on a snowy day." David didn't even check his references. That is the kind of person you want in charge of your bodyguard. Lion chasers make great bouncers.

Now zoom out and look at the story through a wide-angled lens.

Most people would have seen the lion as a five-hundred-pound problem, but not Benaiah. For most people, finding yourself in a pit with a lion on a snowy day would qualify as bad luck. But can you see how God turned what could have been considered a *bad break* into a *big break*? Benaiah lands a job interview with the King of Israel.

I'm sure the bodyguard position was the last thing on his mind when he encountered the lion, but Benaiah wasn't just chasing a lion. Benaiah was chasing a position in David's administration.

Here's the point: God is in the résumé-building business. He is always using past experiences to prepare us for future opportunities. But those God-given opportunities often come disguised as man-eating lions. And how we react when we encounter those lions will determine our destiny. We can cower in fear and run away from our greatest challenges. Or we can chase our God-ordained destiny by seizing the God-ordained opportunity.

As I look back on my own life, I recognize this simple truth: The greatest opportunities were the scariest lions. Part of me has wanted to play it safe, but I've learned that taking no risks is the greatest risk of all.

Giving up a full-ride scholarship at the University of Chicago to transfer to a small Bible college was a huge risk. Asking my wife, Lora, to marry me was a huge risk. (Of course, not as big a risk as Lora saying yes!) Packing all of our earthly belongings into a fifteen-foot U-haul and moving to Washington DC with no place to live and no guaranteed salary was a huge risk. Each of our three children was a huge risk. Jumping into a church plant with zero pastoral experience was a huge risk, both for me and for the church.

But when I look in the rearview mirror, I realize that the biggest risks were the greatest opportunities. Some of those life-altering decisions caused sleepless nights. The steps of faith were accompanied by acute fear that caused nausea. We experienced some financial hardships that required miraculous provision. And we had to pick ourselves up and dust ourselves off after falling flat on our faces a few times.

isn't that what I want?
✓ *what I felt in Rwanda, even though it was scary*

But those were the moments that I came alive. Those were the moments when God set the stage. Those were the moments that changed the trajectory of my life.

NO GUTS, NO GLORY

In his book *If Only*,[1] Dr. Neal Roese makes a fascinating distinction between two types of regret: regrets of action and regrets of inaction. A regret of action is "wishing you hadn't done something." In theological terms, it's called a *sin of commission*. A regret of inaction is "wishing you had done something." In theological terms, it's a *sin of omission*.

I think the church has fixated on sins of commission for far too long. We have a long list of *don'ts*. Think of it as holiness by subtraction. We think holiness is the byproduct of subtracting something from our lives that shouldn't be there. And holiness certainly involves subtraction. But I think God is more concerned about sins of omission—those things we could have and should have done. It's holiness by multiplication. Goodness is not the absence of badness. You can do nothing wrong and still do nothing right. Those who simply run away from sin are half-Christians. Our calling is much higher than simply running away from what's wrong. We're called to chase lions.

There is an old aphorism: "No guts, no glory." When we don't have the guts to step out in faith and chase lions, then God is robbed of the glory that rightfully belongs to Him.

Is anybody else tired of reactive Christianity that is more known for what it's against than what it's for? We've become far too defensive. We've become far too passive. Lion chasers are proactive. They know that playing it safe is risky. Lion chasers are always on the lookout for God-ordained opportunities.

Maybe we've measured spiritual maturity the wrong way. Maybe following Christ isn't supposed to be as *safe* or as *civilized* as we've been led to believe. Maybe Christ was more *dangerous* and *uncivilized* than our Sunday-school flannelgraphs portrayed. Maybe God is raising up a generation of lion chasers.

In this book, I will introduce you to some of the lion chasers I know. People like John, a Georgetown lawyer who put his law practice on hold to shoot a documentary film about human trafficking in Uganda. Or Kurt, a tenured professor who gave up his chair to pursue a dot-com dream. Or Natalie, a college grad who moved halfway around the world to teach English in the Marshall Islands. Or Sarah, an NCCer who followed God's leading to a mission trip in Ethiopa, despite her many fears. Or Lee, who not only quit his executive-level position at Microsoft but forfeited all of his stock options to plant a church. Or Greg, a political neophyte who decided to throw his hat in the ring and run for a congressional seat.

Most of us applaud lion chasers from the sidelines. *Good for them!* We're inspired by people who face their fears and chase their dreams. What we fail to realize is that they are no different from us.

The lion chasers you'll meet in this book are ordinary people. They put their pants on one leg at a time like everybody else. Most of them were scared to death when they bought the plane ticket or handed in their resignation. Weighing the pros and cons caused some ulcers along the way. And at times it felt like *they* were the ones cornered by the lion in the snowy pit.

I wish I could tell you that every lion chase ends with a lion skin hanging on the wall, but it doesn't. The dot-com dreamer is successful beyond his wildest dreams, but the guy with political aspirations lost the election. However, both of them are lion chasers in my book. What sets lion chasers apart isn't the outcome. It's the courage to chase God-sized dreams. Lion chasers don't let their fears or doubts keep them from doing what God has called them to do.

A SURVIVAL GUIDE FOR LION CHASERS

I have a simple definition of success: <u>Do the best you can with what you have where you are</u>. In essence, success is making the most of every opportunity. Spiritual maturity is *seeing and seizing God-ordained opportunities*. Think of every opportunity as God's gift to you. <u>What you do with those opportunities is your gift to God</u>. I'm absolutely convinced that our greatest regrets in life will be missed opportunities.

At the end of the day, *success equals stewardship* and *stewardship equals success*. But our view of stewardship is far too parochial. Sure, how we manage our time, talent, and treasure is a huge stewardship issue. But what about being a good steward of our imagination? Or our medial ventral prefrontal cortex (the seat of humor, according to neurologists)? Or how about stewardship of our sex drive and competitive streaks? Stewardship is all-inclusive. We've got to be good stewards of every second of time and every ounce of energy. But right at the top of the stewardship list is what I'd call *opportunity stewardship*.

When you cross paths with the lion, are you going to run away like a scaredy-cat or are you going to grab life by the mane?

Lion chasers grab life by the mane.

Benaiah went on to have a brilliant military career. In fact, he climbed all the way up the chain of command to become commander in chief of Israel's army. But it all started with what many would consider being in the wrong place at the wrong time. His genealogy of success can be traced all the way back to a life-or-death encounter with a man-eating lion. It was fight or flight. Benaiah was faced with a choice that would determine his destiny: run away or give chase.

Not much has changed in the past three thousand years.

I seriously doubt that anybody reading this book will ever find themselves in a pit with a lion on a snowy day. None of us lie awake at night worrying about what we would do in a lion encounter. In a strictly literal sense, can you imagine a more irrelevant topic for a book?

But in a figurative sense, I can't imagine anything more germane.

I don't pretend to know the unique circumstances of your life, but I'm guessing you have encountered some lions, fallen into some pits, and weathered a few snowy days. Maybe it's a God-sized dream that scares the living daylights out of you. Maybe a bad habit or a bad decision finds you at the bottom of a pit. Or maybe a cloud of self-doubt casts a dark shadow on your future.

Think of *In a Pit With a Lion on a Snowy Day* as a survival guide for lion chasers. As you strap on Benaiah's sandals and unsheathe his sword, you'll learn *seven skills* that will help you climb out of the slipperiest pits and chase the biggest lions.

Some of the skills will come naturally for certain personality types. If you're optimistic by nature, *overcoming adversity* will come more easily. If you tend toward the pessimistic end of the spectrum, it will require more intentionality.

Some skills will feel as unnatural as writing with your weak hand or rapelling off a cliff for the first time. *Unlearning fears* and *embracing uncertainty* requires a counterintuitive approach to life. But like Benaiah, the courage to swim against the current will help you get where God wants you to go.

Some skills, like *calculating risks* or *seizing opportunities*, are developmental and habitual. Almost like innate athletic ability or musical prowess, practice makes perfect. The more risks you take, the easier it becomes. Seizing opportunities becomes second nature. *Defying odds* and *looking foolish* will become default settings.

I don't know where you are geographically or demographically. I'm not sure how you're doing emotionally, physically, relationally, and spiritually. But these skills will help you get where God wants you to go—no matter where you're starting from. The principles in this book aren't just a script out of Scripture. They can rewrite the story of your life. All you have to do is turn the page and begin a new chapter.

CHAPTER 1 REVIEW

Points to Remember

- God is in the business of strategically positioning us in the right place at the right time. But the right place often seems like the *wrong* place, and the right time often seems like the *wrong* time.
- Goodness is not the absence of badness. You can do nothing wrong and still do nothing right. Our calling is much higher than simply running away from what's wrong. We're called to chase lions—look for opportunities in our problems and obstacles, and take risks to reach for God's best.
- When we don't have the guts to step out in faith and chase lions, then God is robbed of the glory that rightfully belongs to Him.
- Spiritual maturity is seeing and seizing God-ordained opportunities.

Starting Your Chase

Based on what you've read so far, which lion-chasing skills do you think might be most difficult for you to master?

Defying odds?
- Facing fears?
Reframing problems?
- Embracing uncertainty?
- Taking risks?
Seizing opportunities?
- Looking foolish?

The Odd Thing About Odds

How much happier you would be,
how much more of you there would be,
if the hammer of a higher God
could smash your small cosmos.

G.K. CHESTERTON

I'm not sure what kind of line Jerusalem oddsmakers would have given the three incidents recorded in 2 Samuel 23, but I do know this: Benaiah *wasn't* the odds-on favorite.

Benaiah had to be a two-to-one underdog when he fought two of Moab's mightiest warriors. This wasn't a tag-team wrestling match. Benaiah was double-teamed.

I'm guessing the Egyptian giant was at least a ten-to-one favorite. For starters, Benaiah had a club and the Egyptian had a spear the size of a weaver's rod. If I'm placing bets on a club or a spear, I put my money on the sharp, pointy spear every time! But the weapon advantage is only part of the disparity. According to Scripture, the Egyptian was seven and a half feet tall. In the boxing world, the tale of the tape is a major factor in who is favored to win a fight. A fighter with a longer reach has a distinct advantage over a shorter boxer. Given his height, I'm guessing the Egyptian had an eighteen- to twenty-four-inch reach advantage. Add the weapon advantage and size advantage together and you've got a mismatch the size of David versus Goliath. I want to see the instant replay of Benaiah wrenching the spear out of the Egyptian's giant hands. How did he even get close enough to grab it?

And then there is the epic encounter with a lion in a pit on a snowy day. Scripture is silent on whether or not Benaiah even had a weapon. But even if he did, it wasn't a hunting rifle. This was hand-to-paw combat. And once again, Benaiah had a significant physical disadvantage. A fully grown male lion weighs hundreds of pounds more, runs many miles per hour faster, and leaps much farther than any man. Its jaws are powerful enough to bite through skull bones, and its canine teeth are used to rip through animal hides. And considering the fact that lions hunt everything from wildebeests to giraffes, Benaiah is small prey. He's nothing more than a light hors d'oeuvres before the main course. But along with the physical disadvantages, you've got to factor in topographical and meteorological factors. I would definitely give the lion home-field advantage. A pit is a lion's domain. A lion's eyesight is five times better than a human with twenty-twenty vision, giving the lion a significant advantage in a poorly lit pit. And a sure-footed lion with catlike reflexes certainly gains the upper paw in snowy, slippery conditions. Add it all together and Benaiah had to be a hundred-to-one long shot.

But Benaiah did what lion chasers do. He defied the odds. He didn't focus on his disadvantages. He didn't make excuses. He didn't try to avoid situations where the odds were against him. Lion chasers know God is bigger and more powerful than any problem they face in this world. They thrive in the toughest circumstances because they know that impossible odds set the stage for amazing miracles. That is how God reveals his glory—and how He blesses you in ways you never could have imagined.

IMPOSSIBLE ODDS

There is a pattern that I see repeated throughout Scripture: Sometimes God won't intervene until something is humanly impossible. And He usually does it just in the nick of time. I think that pattern reveals one dimension of God's personality: God loves impossible odds. And I can relate to that.

One of the most exhilarating things in the world is doing something that no one thinks you can do. As a kid I turned everything into a challenge. It didn't matter whether we were driving in the car, taking a bike ride, or eating dinner. *Do you think I can hold my breath through the tunnel? Do you think I can do a pop-a-wheelie to the end of the block? Do you think I can eat a kitchen-sink ice cream sundae in thirty seconds?*

If someone said yes, I wouldn't even bother trying. What's the point of doing something that someone already thinks you can do? So I'd up the ante or raise the stakes until no one thought it was possible. Then I would attempt the impossible. Is there any greater high than doing what no one thinks you can do?

Maybe that is why God sometimes invites us to defy impossible odds. Maybe it is one way He can show us His omnipotence. Maybe God allows the odds to be stacked against us so He can reveal more of His glory.

I think that explains the counterintuitive military strategy in Judges 6. Gideon's army of thirty-two thousand men is vastly outnumbered by the Midianites. They are already underdogs when the Lord gives a counterintuitive command: "You have too many men for me to deliver Midian into their hands."

What? If I'm Gideon, I'm thinking God misspoke. *You said "too many," but I think you really meant to say "too few."*

But God tells Gideon to discharge anyone who is afraid, and Gideon loses two-thirds of his army. Now he's down to ten thousand men, and the oddsmakers adjust the point spread.

Then the Lord says it again: "There are still too many men."

Gideon wants God to call for a draft, but God devises a test to get rid of even more foot soldiers. Gideon's army goes to get a drink of water, and God tells him to dismiss the men who drink like a dog. That leaves Gideon with an "army" of three hundred men.

The odds had to be a million to one at this point. But it gets even better! God tells Gideon to attack the Midianites with trumpets and jars. *You've got to be kidding me!* What kind of battle plan is that?

And here's the kicker: *Israel wins!*

So why does God do it that way?

"You have too many warriors with you. If I let all of you fight the Midianites, the Israelites will boast to me that they saved themselves by their own strength."

If Gideon had attacked with thirty-two thousand men and won, I'm pretty sure the Israelites would have thanked God for *lending them a hand,* and God would have gotten partial credit. But that's not what God wants or deserves. God wants and deserves full credit. And when three hundred men defeat a vast army with trumpets and jars, God gets all the glory. Why? Because a victory like that defies all odds.

I know this for sure: Benaiah knew who to praise after defeating the Moabites. He gave God all the props after defeating the Egyptian giant. And he must have had revival in that snowy pit after killing the lion.

Too often our prayers revolve around asking God to reduce the odds in our lives. We want everything in our favor. But maybe God wants to stack the odds against us so we can experience a miracle of divine proportions. Maybe faith is trusting God no matter how impossible the odds are. Maybe our impossible situations are opportunities to experience a new dimension of God's glory.

FOUR-DIMENSIONAL GOD

Here is the mistake most of us make when it comes to God: We think of Him in four-dimensional terms. But God is omni-dimensional.

I was at the White House for a garden tour a few years ago, and I'll never forget walking by a woman that looked totally overwhelmed. I had just passed through security on the way in, and she was on the way out. Following in her wake was a large group of teenage girls, and I could tell by the look on her face that she was their chaperone. For whatever reason, as we passed each other, she said to me: "Keeping track of seventy-nine girls is impossible!"

I know what she means. I can hardly keep track of our three kids at Chuck E. Cheese.

And then I think about God.

How do you keep track of six billion people at the same time? How do you process millions of simultaneous prayer requests—especially those of the fans of different football teams on Super Bowl Sunday or of voters on opposite sides of the political aisle on election day?

I know this for sure: You don't do it in four dimensions.

I am limited to three space dimensions, which simply means that I can only be in one place at one time. And I am limited to one time dimension, which means that I am stuck in a moment and I can't get out of it. I cannot travel into the past or the future because, in one dimension, time is linear. But God is everywhere all the time.

Now the earth was formless and empty, darkness was over the surface of the deep, and the Spirit of God was hovering over the waters.

In the beginning, the Spirit of God was hovering over the chaos. And nothing has changed. God is still hovering over chaos. The creation story is a microcosm of what God wants to do in your life. He hovers over the chaotic situations ready to create order and beauty. He wants to fill the void.

The word *over* in the phrase "over the water" comes from the two-dimensional Hebrew word *paniym*. In regards to time, paniym can refer to the split second before something happens and the split second after something happens. In regards to space, it can refer to the space right in front or right in back of you.

In the words of the Psalmist:

I look behind me and you're there, then up ahead and you're there too.

It's almost as if God forms a parenthesis in time and a parenthesis in space around us. He is hovering all around you all the time.

Let me try to put it in scientific terms. The shortest possible time is 10^{-43} seconds. It is called Planck time. Any shorter and quantum mechanics can't tell whether events are simultaneous. The shortest possible distance is 1.6×10^{-35} meters. It's called Planck length. Any shorter and quantum mechanics can't distinguish between here and there.

And that's where God comes in. He's in the space and the time that, according to quantum mechanics, doesn't exist.

To finite human beings, time and space seem infinite, but that is because we're on the inside looking out. God is on the outside looking in. Time and space are a finite part of His creation. That's why "a day is like a thousand years, and a thousand years are like a day." God is all around us all the time. He is right before, right after, right ahead, and right behind. God has no dimensional limitations, and if we could wrap our minds around that truth, it would transform our outlook on life.

Mathematicians refer to each space-time dimension as "a degree of freedom." In very simplistic terms, a dimension is a way you can move. And the number of dimensions determines what is and what is not possible. The more dimensions, the more freedom you have. You can jump over a four-dimensional wall in five-dimensional space or untangle a seven-dimensional knot in eight-dimensional space. Add a time dimension or space dimension, and a universe of possibilities opens up to us.

Think of it in terms of a newspaper comic. In a sense, comic-strip characters are prisoners of two dimensions. They can move horizontally and vertically, but they cannot escape the two-dimensional surface of the paper. They are stuck in those little comic strip boxes. But imagine if a comic strip character could take on a third dimension. The added degree of freedom would enable him to jump right off the page.

Isn't that what faith does? Maybe we underestimate our *freedom* in Christ. Maybe it's not just freedom from sin. Maybe it is the freedom to do the extradimensional.

Faith gives us the dimensional freedom to overcome our human limitations by exiting space-time via prayer.

A High View of God

According to A. W. Tozer, the most important thing about you is what comes to mind when you think about God.

> ...the most portentous fact about any man is not what he at a given time may say or do, but what he in his deep heart conceives God to be like....
>
> Were we able to extract from any man a complete answer to the question, "What comes to your mind when you think about God?" we might predict with certainty the spiritual future of that man.[2]

Interesting idea

How you think about God will determine who you become. You aren't just the byproduct of "nature" and "nurture." You are a byproduct of your God-picture. And that internal picture of God determines how you see everything else.

Most of our problems are not circumstantial. Most of our problems are perceptual. Our biggest problems can be traced back to an inadequate understanding of who God is. Our problems seem really big because our God seems really small. In fact, we reduce God to the size of our biggest problem.

Tozer said a "low view of God...is the cause of a hundred lesser evils." But a person with a high view of God "is relieved of ten thousand temporal problems."[3]

A low view of God and a high view of God are the difference between scaredy-cats and lion chasers. Scaredy-cats are filled with fear because their God is so small. Lion chasers know that their best thought about God on their best day falls infinitely short of how great God really is.

> "My thoughts are not your thoughts, neither are my ways your ways," declares the LORD. "As the heavens are higher than the earth so are my ways higher than your ways and my thoughts than your thoughts."

Astronomers have spied galaxies 12.3 billion light-years from earth. To put that distance into perspective, consider the fact that light traveling 186,000 miles per second only takes eight minutes to travel the 93 million miles between the sun and planet earth. Sunlight is only eight minutes old. But light from the furthest galaxy takes 12.3 billion years to get here. That distance is virtually incomprehensible! And God says that is about the distance between His thoughts and our thoughts. Your best thought about God on your best day falls

12.3 billion light-years short of how great and how good God really is. We underestimate God's goodness and greatness by at least 12.3 billion light-years.

You know what the greatest tragedy in life is? It is someone whose god gets smaller and smaller with each passing day.

Maybe it's time to stop placing four-dimensional limits on God. Maybe it's time to stop putting God in a box the size of your cerebral cortex. Maybe it's time to stop creating God in your image and let Him create you in His.

The more we grow, the bigger God should get. And the bigger God gets, the smaller our lions will become.

Contingency Plans

Long before God laid earth's foundations, he had us in mind. Long, long ago he decided to adopt us into his family. He thought of everything, provided for everything we could possibly need.

Translation: God planned for every contingency you might ever encounter, before the beginning of time.

That is one of the most mind-boggling truths in Scripture. It is impossible for finite minds to comprehend the sovereignty of God, but let me put it in chess terms.

In 1997, a team of IBM engineers designed and developed Deep Blue, the computer that outmaneuvered chess grand master Garry Kasparov. Deep Blue was equipped with thirty-two processing engines that could calculate 200 million chess moves per second.

I don't know about you, but I have a tough time with the fifty-fifty stuff. True or false. Right or left. Chocolate or vanilla. I can't even imagine contemplating 200 million contingencies in a split second. But 200 million contingencies is laughable compared to the Omniscient One who took every contingency into consideration before a nanosecond had even ticked off the clock of time.

Think of your life as a game of chess. You are the pawn and God is the Grand Master. You have no idea what your next move should be, but God already has the next 200 million moves planned out. Some of His moves won't make sense, but that is simply because we can't compute 200 million contingencies at a time! We've just got to trust the Grand Master.

Whenever I counsel someone who is wrestling with discerning the will of God, I remind them of this simple truth: <u>God wants you to get where God wants you to go more than you want to get where God wants you to go</u>. Read that again if you need to. It ought to relieve your tension headaches. If you keep in step with the Spirit, God is going to make sure you get where He wants you to go. He is always working behind the scenes, engineering our circumstances and setting us up for success.

We are God's workmanship, created in Christ Jesus to do good works, which God prepared in advance for us to do.

The word *prepared* derives from an ancient custom of sending servants ahead of a king to secure safe passage. But God turns the tables. The King of Kings goes in advance of His servants and prepares the road ahead for *us*.

Now here's the catch: Sometimes His itinerary entails coming face to face with a lion in a pit on a snowy day. But when you find yourself in those challenging circumstances, you need to know that God is ordering your footsteps. You can have a sense of destiny because you know that God has considered every contingency in your life, and He always has your best interest at heart. And that sense of destiny, rooted in the sovereignty of God, helps you pray the unthinkable and attempt the impossible.

TO THE INFINITE ALL
FINITES ARE EQUAL

Second Kings 6 records what may be the most ridiculous prayer in Scripture. A group of prophets are chopping trees near a river and one of their iron ax heads falls into the river. The prophet who lost the ax head said to Elisha: "Alas, master! For it was borrowed."

Notice the verb tense. This apprentice uses the past tense. As far as he's concerned, this ax head is as good as gone. It reminds me of one of Jack Handey's Deep Thoughts: *If you drop your keys in a river of molten lava, let 'em go man, 'cause they're gone!*

If you drop your iron ax head in the river, let it go man, 'cause it's gone!

This apprentice regarded his loss as final. He had no expectation whatsoever that the ax head would be retrieved. I think he wanted a little mercy or a little sympathy, but he wasn't expecting a miracle. He didn't even have a category for what was about to happen, and there is good reason. Any mineral with a density greater than one gram per cubic centimeter doesn't float. The density of cast iron is approximately 7.2 grams per cubic centimeter.

Translation: Iron ax heads don't float.

Or do they?

There is only one way to find out: Pray a ridiculous prayer!

Now here is what I love about this story. If I'm Elisha, I feel bad for the guy who lost the borrowed ax head. Maybe I let him borrow mine. Maybe I drive him to the hardware store to get a new one. But it doesn't even cross my mind to pray that it would float. But you can tell the wheels are turning in Elisha's mind because he asks where the ax head fell in. If I'm the apprentice, I'm thinking, *What difference does it make?* But he shows Elisha where he lost it. Elisha cuts a stick and throws it into the water, and something happens that had probably never happened before and has never happened since.

And the iron did swim.

This ranks as one of my favorite miracles in Scripture for a couple reasons. First, this isn't a life-or-death situation. Yes, it's a borrowed ax head. Yes, he lost it. But if that is the worst thing that's ever happened to you, you've led a pretty sheltered life. You know what I'm saying? It's an *ax head*. This may sound crazy, but doesn't it seem like maybe you ought to save an amazing miracle like this for a little bigger tragedy? But I would put this miracle in the category of Jesus turning water into wine at a wedding party. Why waste your first miracle on helping a bride and groom save face because they didn't stock enough wine for the reception? But I think this reveals something about God. He cares about the little things like wedding receptions and borrowed ax heads. God is great not just because nothing is too big for Him. God is great but because nothing is too small for Him either.

The other reason I love this miracle is because it was such a ridiculous request. Elisha had to feel a little funny even verbalizing this prayer:

Dear God, I know that iron ax heads have a density of 7.2 grams per cubic centimeter. I know that at body temperature, no liquid has a viscosity as low as water. But would you consider defying the laws of physics and doing what has never been done before? Please make this iron ax head swim.

These kinds of miracles help us redefine reality. And the reality is that nothing is too difficult for God.

Degree of Difficulty

We tend to rank miracles. Almost like a judge at a gymnastics competition that ranks a routine based on degree of difficulty, we rank our prayer requests. We have *big* requests and *little* requests. We have *easy* requests and *difficult* requests. But that is a false construct. The truth is this: *To the infinite all finites are equal.* There is no big or small, easy or difficult, possible or impossible. When it comes to God, there are no degrees of difficulty. There are no odds when it comes to God. All bets are off.

What were the odds of Jesus feeding five thousand people with five loaves and two fish? Let's just say each loaf of bread or each fish is equal to one meal. Then I'm guessing the odds were approximately five thousand to seven. And to the disciples, that seemed like an insurmountable problem: "Eight months' wages would not buy enough bread for each one to have a bite!"

You can almost see the disciples trying to crunch the numbers, but any way you slice five loaves and filet two fish, you still come up 4,993 meals short. It just doesn't add up. $5 + 2 = 7$.

Jesus then took the loaves, gave thanks, and distributed them to those who were seated as much as they wanted. He did the same with the fish. When they had all had enough to eat, he said to his disciples, "Gather the pieces that are left over. Let nothing be wasted." So they gathered them and filled twelve baskets with the pieces of the five barley loaves left over by those who had eaten.

In God's economy, $5 + 2 = 5,000$ with a remainder of 12.

They actually end up with more than what they started with after feeding five thousand people. And God is glorified because He defied impossible odds.

It honestly doesn't matter how many Moabites you're facing. It doesn't matter how tall the Egyptian giant is. And the size of the lion isn't really the issue.

The issue is this: *How big is your God?*

Ridiculous Prayers

Because we know the outcome of the lion chase, we fail to appreciate the way it looked to the average bystander. What if Benaiah had been killed by the lion? Let's just say it like it is: He would have looked completely ridiculous. Can't you hear people whispering under their breath at the funeral? *What was Benaiah thinking?* But lion chasers aren't afraid of doing something that seems ridiculous to others—because they know *anything* is possible with God. A request can never be too ridiculous when you're asking the One who knows no limits.

When National Community Church was just getting off the ground, we started praying a ridiculous prayer. We prayed that God would give us a piece of property half a block from Union Station. At the time, it was a graffiti-covered nuisance property. Actually, in its heyday, it was used as a crack house. But I could envision a first-class, fully operational coffeehouse on that corner. So we started praying. I did prayer walks around the property. We laid hands on the building. And I prayed for it every time I walked by it.

It was a ridiculous prayer for a number of reasons. First of all, we couldn't afford it. The original asking price was one million dollars, and we didn't have the attendance or giving to finance that kind of dream eight years ago. Secondly, churches build churches. They don't typically build coffeehouses. Plus, we had zero experience in the coffeehouse business. And finally, the owners were courting Starbucks. The odds were definitely stacked against us.

I still remember my first phone call to the owners of the property. I felt foolish even calling them. I felt awkward. I felt nervous. I felt young. And I had no idea what to say. We really had no business pursuing the property, but we dared to dream a God-sized dream. And six years after praying a ridiculous prayer, we purchased lot 109 in square 754 in the District of Columbia. The entire process was so full of divine interventions that we named the coffeehouse Ebenezers, which means "hitherto hath the LORD helped us." That ridiculous prayer is now the largest coffeehouse in Washington DC. It is also one of the nicest and busiest. It doesn't hurt that it is strategically located in the shadow of Union Station, across the street from the Federal Judiciary Building, kitty-corner to Station Place, the largest office building in Washington DC, and it forms the northwest corner of the Capitol Hill Historic District.

Now, here is the amazing thing. Right after purchasing the property, four different neighbors told me that they had offered more money than we did. I'm neither a real estate agent nor the son of a real estate agent, but don't you typically sell to the highest bidder? The only explanation I have is the favor of God. God had His hand on the property, and He wouldn't allow anyone else to purchase it.

"Whatever you bind on earth will be bound in heaven, and whatever you loose on earth will be loosed in heaven."

We underestimate how much spiritual authority we have when we pray in accordance with the will of God. The word *bind* means "to prohibit or to fasten with chains." When we exercised our spiritual authority in prayer and laid hands on that property, it was like our prayers put a spiritual chain link fence around 201 F Street, NE. And God prohibited anyone from buying it for more than two decades.

In fact, I met a neighbor not long after our coffeehouse opened up who said: "If it weren't for me, you wouldn't have a coffeehouse." He went on to explain that he has lived in the neighborhood for more than twenty-five years. And back in the 1980s, when the former owners of our property applied for a demolition permit, this neighbor stopped them. He went to the historic preservation society and got the property deemed a historic property. And if he hadn't done what he did, a fast-food chain or dry cleaner would have snapped up the property before we even moved into the neighborhood. Long before the dream of building a coffeehouse was even conceived, God had a contract on that property.

THE SCROLL OF REMEMBRANCE

You may be thinking, *Even if God is great enough to do absolutely anything, why would He answer my prayer? Why would he do a miraculous thing through me?* Well, when you come right down to it, God is more than a Grand Master, more than a time traveler, more than a lot of scientific theories. He's our *Father.*

Sometimes I watch my kids without them knowing that I'm watching them. I love to watch them playing when they are in the zone. I love to walk by their school classrooms and watch them in their natural habitat. And I love coming into their rooms at night when they're sound asleep and watching them. Sometimes I watch them because I'm concerned about them. Sometimes I watch them because I'm proud of them. Sometimes I watch them because I know they're going to do what I told them *not* to do. And sometimes I watch them because I just love watching them. I can see myself in my children.

Like a loving parent, our Heavenly Father loves watching his children. In fact, God isn't just watching. He is actually scrapbooking. Scripture calls it "a scroll of remembrance." God is recording absolutely every act of righteousness. That includes the secret things no one sees and the small things no one notices. Nothing you do right will go unrewarded. And God isn't just recording those acts of righteousness. He is rejoicing over you the way a parent rejoices over a child.

Please don't miss or dismiss this simple truth: God is a proud parent. You are "the apple of his eye." And our Heavenly Father celebrates every accomplishment. But I've got to think that nothing brings God greater joy than when one of His children defies the odds.

One of my most memorable moments as a parent happened during my son Parker's rookie season in little league basketball. His team hadn't won a single game all season. And we lost this particular game forty to five. Unfortunately, that's not a misprint. But there was a silver lining. One of the five points was scored by my son. And it was nothing short of miraculous.

I'd been practicing free throws with Parker since the season started, and he never, I repeat *never*, made one. He just wasn't strong enough yet to shoot a regulation ball fifteen feet through a basket on a ten-foot-high rim. In two months of practice, he'd only hit the rim a couple times. He had a 98 percent air-ball percentage from the free throw line.

So Parker got fouled and went to the free throw line. And to be perfectly honest, I felt bad at first because I knew my son had a 98 percent chance of being embarrassed. But I prayed like it was the day of Pentecost! I wish I could say that I prayed that Parker would make the free throw, but I didn't have that much faith. I just prayed that he would hit the rim. But Parker stepped up to the free throw line and renewed my faith in the power of prayer. Parker defied the odds and made the first free throw of his short and unillustrious basketball career.

And I cried.

I'm not kidding! I cried tears of joy. I tried to maintain my composure because it seems sort of silly to cheer too loud when you're losing so badly to the other team. But I had personal revival. It was a holy moment. I think I got more excited about Parker's first free throw than all the shots I made in my college basketball career combined.

Why? Because I'm a normal parent. And parents rejoice when their children do something right. Our Heavenly Father is no exception. In fact, He sets the standard for the rest of us to follow.

Trust me, God was a lot more excited about Benaiah chasing and killing the lion than Benaiah was. I can see Him ribbing one of the angels and saying: "Did you see what my boy Benaiah did?"

Lion chasers defy the odds—and make their Father proud.

Chapter 2 Review

Points to Remember

- Lion chasers thrive in the toughest circumstances because they know that impossible odds set the stage for amazing miracles.
- The mistake most of us make when it comes to God is that we think He is four-dimensional. But God has no dimensional limits.
- How you think of God will determine who you become.
- God is always working behind the scenes, engineering our circumstances and setting us up for success.
- The more we grow, the bigger God should get. And the bigger God gets, the smaller our lions become.
- The reality is that *nothing* is too difficult for God.

Starting Your Chase

How big is your God? Is He big enough to do anything, or are there limits (in your mind) to what God can do? What could you do today to begin to live with a bigger, better view of God?

CHAPTER 3

Unlearning Your Fears

The price of our vitality is the sum of our fears.
DAVID WHYTE

It was about a year ago that I was part of a team of NCCers that went on a mission trip to Ethiopia. We helped plant a church in the capitol city of Addis Ababa, and we went to serve the church in a variety of capacities. That week was full of unforgettable experiences. We built a mud hut for an Ethiopian grandmother. We played Duck, Duck, Goose with kids in an elementary school. And I had the opportunity to preach to thousands of Ethiopian believers who worship God with a spiritual intensity I've rarely seen in America.

Before going on the trip, everybody on the team was a little nervous. It was during a time of political unrest, we were subjecting ourselves to a variety of third-world diseases, and even drinking the water and eating the food was done conscientiously. So all of us were anxious, but one team member, Sarah, was downright fearful—especially when she learned that we were going to camp out in Awash National Park. Somehow, knowing that armed guards would keep watch all night didn't ease her mind. Neither did the crocodiles we saw in the river or the lions we heard from around the campfire.

But I was so proud of her. Sarah faced her fear. She trusted her team. She genuinely believed that God was calling her to go on that trip. And because she pushed through her fears, she experienced some of the most amazing memories. She decided to live her life in a way that was worth telling stories about:

There were a million reasons why I shouldn't go. I'm not an evangelist. I don't have any special talents. I don't have three thousand dollars lying around. I've never been west of the Mississippi River, much less out of the Western Hemisphere. I'm not a physically ambitious person. I can't survive without electricity or running water. But I only needed one reason to go: I was called.

In retrospect, it's hard to imagine how many memories she would have forfeited if she had run away from her fears. We drove through the Ethiopian outback and went swimming in a natural spring that was heated by a volcano. You don't get to do that every day. We visited a tribal village that looked like it came right out of the pages of National Geographic. None of us will forget our game drive on top of Land Rovers. With the African sun beating down on us and the breeze in our faces, we saw animals we'd never even seen in a zoo. Then we stopped at a little café overlooking the Awash River. It was the kind of view that required a moment of silence. As I looked over that cliff that dropped two hundred feet straight down, I could sense the Spirit of God saying to my spirit: Look at what I made! It was one of the most spiritual moments of my life. I could literally sense God enjoying how much we were enjoying His creation.

I'll never forget blogging in my pup tent that night. (I'm sure our guards were rather curious about the iridescent glow emanating from my tent.) I remember writing these words: "Don't accumulate possessions; accumulate experiences!"

Then I turned off my computer and started thanking God for absolutely everything that happened that day. I thanked Him for the camels and baboons and warthogs. I actually named all the animals I had seen. I thanked Him for the waterfall and the mountains. I even thanked Him for the armed shepherds carrying AK-47s who wanted money for the pictures we took of their cattle. I relived the entire day in prayer. Then I fell asleep. Not a bad way to end one of the most unbelievable days of my life.

Now here is my point. What if Sarah had let fear keep her from going on the trip? Think of how many amazing experiences she would have forfeited. Think of the memories that would have been lost. Think of the stories that would have gone untold.

For what it's worth, none of the things Sarah was afraid of happened. The plane didn't crash. She didn't get sick. And she wasn't eaten alive by a wild animal. The only bad thing that happened to her was getting pooped on by a baboon. I kid you not! There must have been about fifty baboons of all shapes and sizes hanging out in our campsite. Actually, we were hanging out in *their* campsite. And one of them, high up in a tree, launched a baboon bomb. I'm not sure if the baboon was aiming or not, but what a shot. I know that is nasty. It's gross enough looking at a baboon's bare butt. But what an ice breaker at parties. *Hey, I got pooped on by a baboon once.* How many people do you know who can say that? What a story! That is when you know you're living life to the fullest.

So here is my advice: Don't let mental lions keep you from experiencing everything God has to offer. The greatest breakthroughs in your life will happen when you push through the fear. The defining moments will double as the scariest decisions. But you've got to face those fears and begin the process of unlearning them.

UNLEARNING

Almost like a hard drive with a computer virus, our minds have infected files. Irrational fears and misconceptions keep us from operating the way we were designed to. And if those fears and misconceptions aren't uninstalled, they undermine everything we do.

Half of learning is learning. The other half of learning is unlearning. Unfortunately, unlearning is twice as hard as learning. It's like missing your exit on the freeway. You have to drive to the next exit and then double back. Every mile you go in the wrong direction is really a two-mile error. Unlearning is twice as hard, and it often takes twice as long. It is harder to get old thoughts *out* of your mind than it is to get new thoughts *into* your mind.

That is the challenge Jesus faced, isn't it?

If you study the teachings of Christ, you'll realize that learning wasn't his primary goal. His primary goal was unlearning. He was reverse engineering religious minds. And those can be the toughest minds to change. That is why two phrases are repeated over and over again in the Sermon on the Mount.

"You have heard that it was said..."

"But I tell you..."

What was Jesus saying and doing? He was uninstalling Old Testament concepts and upgrading them with New Testament truths.

"You have heard that it was said, 'Eye for eye, and tooth for tooth.' But I tell you, Do not resist an evil person. If someone strikes you on the cheek, turn to him the other also."

"You have heard that it was said, 'Do not commit adultery.' But I tell you that anyone who looks at a woman lustfully has already committed adultery with her in his heart."

"You have heard that it was said, 'Love your neighbor and
hate your enemy.' But I tell you: Love your enemies and pray
for those who persecute you."

Half of spiritual growth is learning what we don't know. The other
half is unlearning what we do know. And it is the failure to unlearn
irrational fears and misconceptions that keeps us from becoming who
God wants us to be.

The invalid in John 5 is a great example of the importance of
unlearning. He had been crippled for thirty-eight years when Jesus
asked him if he wanted to get well. But the man believed there was
only one way to be healed:

"I have no one to help me into the pool when the water is
stirred. While I am trying to get in, someone else goes down
ahead of me."

This man made an assumption that may have cost him thirty-
eight years! He only had one category for healing. He assumed, based
on ancient superstition, that he had to be the first one into the pool
of Bethesda when the water was stirred in order to be healed. In a
sense, he was imprisoned by what he knew. But Jesus uninstalled that
mistaken belief with one sentence: "Stand up, pick up your sleeping
mat, and walk!"

Now, here is what you need to see. Jesus didn't just set this man
free physically. He set him free cognitively. Faith is unlearning the
senseless worries and misguided beliefs that keep us captive. It is
far more complex than simply modifying behavior. Faith involves
synaptogenesis. Faith is rewiring the human brain.

Neurologically speaking, that is what we do when we study
Scripture. We are literally upgrading our minds by downloading the
mind of Christ.

Do not conform any longer to the pattern of this world, but
be transformed by the renewing of your mind.

Just as a computer hard drive needs to be defragmented to
optimize performance, our minds need to be defragmented. So how
do we defragment our faith? How do we renew our minds? How do
we get ourselves out of the mental pit we've gotten ourselves into? The
way to upgrade your mind is to download Scripture.

Let me put Paul's instructions in neurological context.

Doctors Avi Karni and Leslie Ungerleider of the National Institute
of Mental Health did a fascinating study asking subjects to perform a
simple motor task—a finger-tapping exercise. As subjects tapped, the
doctors conducted an MRI to identify what part of the brain was being
activated. The subjects then practiced the finger-tapping exercise daily
for four weeks. At the end of the four-week period, the brain scan was
repeated. In each instance, it revealed that the area of the brain involved
in the task had expanded. That simple task—a finger-tapping exercise—
literally recruited new nerve cells and rewired neuronal connections.

When we read Scripture, we are recruiting new nerve cells and
rewiring neuronal connections. In a sense, we are downloading a new
operating system that reconfigures the mind. We stop thinking human
thoughts and start thinking God thoughts.

Let this mind be in you which was also in Christ Jesus.

How do we accomplish that command?

Let the word of Christ dwell in you richly.

When we read Scripture, we engage in spiritual tapping. Our
brains are rewired in alignment with the Word, and we develop the
mind of Christ. We think His thoughts.

Facing Fear

Unlearning requires more than just rewiring our brains. We have to use our new knowledge to *face* our fears—and conquer them.

According to psychiatric reference books, there are approximately two thousand classified fears. Those documented fears run the gamut—everything from **triskaidekaphobia (the fear of the number thirteen)** to **arachibutyrophobia (the fear of peanut better sticking to the roof of your mouth)**. There is even a **phobophobia—the fear of acquiring a phobia.**

What's interesting is that psychiatrists posit that we're born with only two innate fears: the fear of falling and the fear of loud noises.

That means that every other fear is learned. And more importantly, that means that every other fear can be *unlearned.*

Our family recently took a little road trip to Nashville, Tennessee, and one of the highlights of our trip was staying at hotels with pools. All three of our kids were super excited, but when we went down to the pool on the first night, our four-year-old, Josiah, refused to get in. I could tell he was afraid, but I couldn't understand why. Then Josiah said, "I don't want to sink." And I had a flashback. The last time we stayed at a hotel with a pool had been a few months before. Josiah was on the stairs in the shallow end when he slipped off and took a serious drink of pool water. He was fine, but it scared him pretty bad. He came over to the hot tub where I was and said, "Dad, I sinked."

Now here's the thing. Josiah loved to swim the summer before. And he was fearless. He would yell, "Dad, catch me," *after* leaping off the edge. But this one scary experience at a hotel pool planted a seed of fear in him.

Honestly, his fear of sinking was totally irrational. I told him I would hold him the entire time, and he could actually touch the bottom. But you can't reason with irrational fears.

I think most of us are shaped, for better or for worse, by a handful of experiences. Those defining experiences can plant a seed of confidence or a seed of doubt, a seed of hope or a seed of helplessness, a seed of faith or a seed of fear.

In this instance, Josiah's sinking experience planted a seed of fear. And it is my job as a parent to pull that emotional weed so Josiah doesn't let an irrational fear of hotel pools take root in his mind. One of my sacred duties as a parent is to help my children unlearn their fears. That is why I took Josiah into the pool against his will. I tried not to traumatize him. And his screaming made me feel like a terrible parent. But I took him into the pool because it is my responsibility as a parent to help my kids face their fears. I knew the fear wouldn't go away if he didn't learn to face it. And I knew he would forfeit so much fun if I didn't help him be brave.

By the way, I also discovered that it is a great way to get a big bear hug. Josiah held on to me like there was no tomorrow!

Don't we have the same experience in our relationship with God? When everything is going great, it's easy to keep our distance. But when we're in fearful situations, we hang on to God for dear life.

Think of your fears as mental lions. If we don't learn to chase those fears, they can keep us at bay for the rest of our lives. So, like a good parent, our Heavenly Father helps us unlearn the fears that would cause us to pass up so much fulfillment and fruitfulness—because He loves us and wants the best for us.

First John 4:18 describes the end goal of our relationship with God: "There is no fear in love. But perfect love drives out fear."

The goal of love is *fearlessness!* As we grow in a love relationship with God, we unlearn the fears that paralyze us and neutralize us spiritually. That is the essence of faith.

Faith is the process of unlearning your irrational fears.

The only God-ordained fear is the fear of God. And if we fear

God, then we don't have to fear anyone or anything else. Unlearning our fears is really a process of learning to trust God more and more.

Faith Allergies

Lion chasers experience the same fears as everyone else. I bet Benaiah was afraid of the boogey man as a kid. But lion chasers have learned to face those fears. They have unlearned the fear of uncertainty, the fear of risk, the fear of looking foolish, and the countless other fears that could hold them back. Their faith has been defragmented. They don't necessarily know more than other people. But they have unlearned the fears that kept them captive. And they all did it the same way: by chasing their fears instead of running away from them. They exposed themselves to the very thing they were afraid of.

Abraham led Isaac to Mount Moriah and placed him on the altar. Moses went back to Pharaoh forty years after running away as a fugitive. And Jesus went into the wilderness to be tempted by Satan himself.

Is there an Isaac you need to sacrifice on the altar? Is there a pharaoh you need to face? Or maybe God is calling you into the wilderness for a season?

Lion chasers don't hide from the things they fear. They chase lions into pits. They expose themselves to the sources of their terror because they know it is the only way to overcome them. Lion chasers have a high threshold for fear because they have built up fear immunity.

I recently went to the doctor's office for an extensive battery of allergy tests. My doctor wanted to find out what allergens trigger my asthma. The nurse-practitioner pricked my forearm in eighteen places with different allergens and said, "Don't scratch." It was like Chinese water torture. I had to resist the urge to scratch the itch for fifteen of the longest minutes of my life!

But testing for allergies isn't a pointless exercise in cruel and unusual punishment, even though it might seem like it. It is a form of reverse engineering. My doctor wasn't satisfied with treating my allergy symptoms. She wanted to discover the root causes of my reactions. And the solution isn't just avoiding those allergens. The cure is actually exposing myself to them in small doses.

Here is my point. The cure for the fear of failure is not success. It's failure. The cure for the fear of rejection is not acceptance. It's rejection. You've got to be exposed to small quantities of whatever you're afraid of. That's how you build up immunity.

When I was in graduate school in the Chicago area, Lora and I wanted to plant a church on Chicago's Northshore. We had a core group. We had a name. We set up a bank account. One minor detail: We never had a service.

That failed attempt was acutely embarrassing because we told everybody that we were going to plant a church, and then we fell flat on our faces. And it was disillusioning because we thought that's what God wanted us to do. It was a complete failure. But it was also one of the best things that ever happened to us. It's not that I like failing any more now than I did then, but somehow that experience released us from the fear of failure. It built up *fear immunity*. So when we had the opportunity to become part of planting National Community Church, we weren't afraid to fail. I figured we couldn't do any more damage than we had done in Chicago!

So what are you afraid of? What allergens trigger a fear reaction? Those are the very things you need to expose yourself to.

One of the greatest things that could happen to you is for your fear to become reality. Then you would discover that it's not the end of the world. Your fear is worse than the actual thing you're afraid of. And if you learn from every mistake, then there is no such thing as failure anyway.

DEFENSELESS

Do you remember the way Scripture describes Satan?

> Your enemy the devil prowls around like a roaring lion looking for someone to devour.

Satan has two primary tactics when it comes to neutralizing you spiritually: discouragement and fear. He wants you to focus on past mistakes you've made. That is why he is called "the accuser of our brethren." And the end result is a loss of courage.

The other tactic is fear. Satan wants to scare the heaven out of you. He wants to put you on your heels so you become reactive and defensive. That is why he is described as a prowling lion.

What we need is a little Christ-like courage to chase the lion.

Jesus never ran away from anyone or anything. He wasn't afraid of walking into the temple when he knew the Pharirazzi had a plot on his life. He wasn't afraid of the lunatic with the legion of demons. And when the lynch mob came to arrest him, what did Jesus do? He didn't run and hide. Scripture says he "stepped forward" and identified himself.

Jesus never ran away from his detractors or persecutors. He chased them.

Even when his life was on the line, Jesus refused to defend himself before the judicial authorities. If he had decided to defend himself,

I'm convinced he could have and would have talked his way out of the
cross. Why? Because he never lost an argument. But he chose instead
to close his mouth and go to the cross.

> He was led like a sheep to the slaughter, and as a lamb before
> the shearer is silent, so he did not open his mouth.

That is the essence of courage, isn't it?
Courage is putting yourself into defenseless positions.
Isn't that what landed Daniel in a lion's den? Isn't that what Esther
did by defying royal protocol and approaching the king without being
summoned? And isn't that what Jesus did on the cross?
The people mocked Jesus. They hurled insults at him. And they
challenged him.

> "If you are the King of the Jews, save yourself."

Can you imagine how difficult it must have been to hear those
words? Because Jesus could have saved himself!

> "Do you think I cannot call on my Father, and he will at once
> put at my disposal more than twelve legions of angels? But
> how then would the Scriptures be fulfilled that say it must
> happen in this way?"

A legion was the largest unit in the Roman military, consisting
of six thousand soldiers. Jesus knew he had more than seventy-two
thousand angels at his disposal. He could have aborted his redemptive
mission with one call for angelic backup. But Jesus wasn't trying to save
himself. He was trying to save you. So he put himself in a defenseless
position. He had the courage to go to the cross.

Time to Take a Stand

There comes a time when you have to face your fears and take a stand for what is right. That is what Shadrach, Meshach, and Abednego did. They risked their lives when they refused to bow down to a ninety-foot idol.

I've got to be honest. I would have been tempted to rationalize compromise in those circumstances. *I'll bow on the outside but not on the inside. I'll cross my fingers while I'm bowing so it doesn't really count. I'll just pretend the idol is Jehovah.* They could have compromised, but lion chasers don't back down. And their acts of courage set the stage for epic miracles.

> Shadrach, Meshach, and Abednego replied to the king, "O Nebuchadnezzar, we do not need to defend ourselves before you in this matter. If we are thrown into the blazing furnace, the God we serve is able to save us from it, and he will rescue us from your hand, O king. But even if he does not, we want you to know, O king, that we will never serve your gods or worship the image of gold you have set up."

I can think of a thousand ways I'd rather die than by fiery furnace! If I had to choose between a lion eating me or a fire burning me, I'm not sure which one I'd choose. But Shadrach, Meshach, and Abednego took a stand. And that is what courage is all about.

Courage is doing what is right regardless of circumstances or consequences.

Shadrach, Meshach, and Abednego refused to defend themselves, and Nebuchadnezzar was so ticked off that he heated the furnace seven times hotter and had them thrown in. It was so hot that the soldiers who threw them into the furnace died. But not a single hair on the head of Shadrach, Meshach, and Abednego was singed.

King Nebuchadnezzar leaped to his feet in amazement and asked his advisers, "Weren't there three men that we tied up and threw into the fire?" They replied, "Certainly, O king." He said, "Look! I see four men walking around in the fire, unbound and unharmed, and the fourth looks like a son of the gods."

When you put yourself into defenseless positions, it sets the stage for God to show up. And that is exactly what happens. Not only do Shadrach, Meshach, and Abednego come out of the fiery furnace alive, they don't even smell like smoke!

What if Shadrach, Meshach, and Abednego had bowed down to the idol?

I'm not sure I can accurately answer that question, but I do know this. They wouldn't have gotten promotions. The Jewish people would not have gotten protected status within the Babylonian kingdom. Idol worship would have continued unabated in Babylon. And Nebuchadnezzar wouldn't have had a life-changing God encounter.

Nebuchadnezzar said, "Praise be to the God of Shadrach, Meshach and Abednego, who has sent his angel and rescued his servants! They trusted in him and defied the king's command and were willing to give up their lives rather than serve or worship any god except their own God. Therefore I decree that the people of any nation or language who say anything against the God of Shadrach, Meshach and Abednego be cut into pieces and their houses be turned into piles of rubble, for no other god can save in this way."

One act of courage by three twentysomethings changed a king and a kingdom.

Maybe it's time to face your fear and take a stand.

THE FUN OF FEAR

Imagine having a conversation with Benaiah over a double shot of espresso. The conversation covers the typical ancient talking points: military strategy, Moabite hygiene, and the latest bodyguard gadgets. Then after some small talk, you ask Benaiah to tell you about the greatest moments of his life. I'm sure Benaiah would recount the three events recorded in 2 Samuel 23. Maybe even embellish a little bit. (Haven't you noticed this universal tendency? The older we get the harder it was and the better we were.)

Then, after getting a blow-by-blow description of his epic acts of courage, you ask Benaiah to tell you about the scariest moments of his life. I'm guessing Benaiah would give you a puzzled look and tell you that he had just told you about them. The greatest moments doubled as the scariest moments. They were one and the same.

It is so easy to read about a lion encounter that happened three thousand years ago and totally underestimate the emotional trauma it must have caused. Most of us have nightmares after seeing something scary on a screen. I guarantee Benaiah woke up in a cold sweat more than once after nocturnal flashbacks. Sure, Benaiah killed the lion. But not before it scared the living daylights out of him! He was a few inches from thirty bared teeth. He could smell the lion's bloody breath. And the sound of the roar echoing in the pit must have echoed in his mind's ear forever.

It was pure fear.

I don't care how battle-tested or battle-scarred you are. I don't care how crazy or courageous you are. You don't come face-to-face with a five-hundred-pound lion without experiencing sheer terror. But the scariest moment of his life turned into the greatest moment of his life.

The same is true for all of us. If you take a second to reflect on your life, you'll discover that the greatest experiences are often the scariest, and the scariest experiences are often the greatest.

That is how life works, isn't it?

I have this question I ask my kids after giving them rocket rides or elevator drops: Was it scary or fun? Usually it is a combination of both. They experience fear when I'm throwing them into the air or dropping them on the couch. But afterwards, it is fun. *Fear, then fun.*

Isn't that why we pay good money to go to theme parks? Sure, we ride the merry-go-round and tea cups. But that isn't why we pay the big bucks. It is the roller coasters with eighty-nine-degree drops that generate the revenue. Have you ever stopped to think about how ironic roller coasters are? We are basically paying someone to scare our stomachs into our throats. We usually get upset at someone who scares us. So why do we pay money to ride roller coasters? Because we have a need for controlled danger. We need a dose of fear every now and then.

It's tough to describe, but there is something about fear that makes us feel alive. The adrenaline is pumping. Your reflexes are catlike. And time stands still. Benaiah must have been scared spitless when he was chasing the lion. But he was never more alive. And it was the fear he felt that made his "in a pit with a lion on a snowy day" story all the more fun to tell ex post facto. The scariest experiences make the best stories, don't they?

So here is my question: *Are you living your life in a way that is worth telling stories about?*

Maybe it is time to quit running and time to start chasing. Try something new. Take some risks. Start doing some things that are worth recounting in jaw-dropping detail. I think we owe it to our kids and grandkids. Imagine the bedtime stories Benaiah must have told his children. I can hear his wife monitoring him. *Remember Benaiah, they're only four and five years old. Keep it G.*

Too many of us pray as if God's primary objective is to keep us from getting scared. But the goal of life is not the elimination of fear. The goal is to muster the moral courage to chase lions.

I'm certainly not suggesting that you jump a fence at your local zoo. Please heed the warning sign on the outside of the lion cage. But I'm concerned that the church has turned into a bunker where we seek shelter when we're actually called to storm the gates of hell. Does that sound safe? I can't imagine a more daring or dangerous mission.

If the truth be told, the alternative to fear is boredom. And boredom isn't just boring. Boredom is inexcusable! Soren Kierkegaard went so far as to say that "boredom is the root of all evil" because it means we're refusing to be who God made us to be. If you're bored, one thing is for sure: You're not following in the footsteps of Christ.

At some point in your life you have to make a choice between fear and boredom.

Lion chasers choose fear.

CHAPTER 3 REVIEW

Points to Remember

- Don't let mental lions keep you from experiencing everything God has to offer.
- Half of spiritual growth is learning what we don't know. The other half is unlearning what we do know.
- It is the failure to unlearn irrational fears and misconceptions that keeps us from becoming who God wants us to be.
- When we read Scripture, our brains are rewired in alignment with the Word, and we develop the mind of Christ.
- The goal of life is not the elimination of fear. The goal is to muster the moral courage to chase lions.

Starting Your Chase

Mark says that "one of the greatest things that can happen to you is for your fear to become a reality." Now that you've read this chapter, do you believe that's true? What fear seems the most overwhelming to you today? What do you think you might gain if that fear became a reality?

The Art of Reframing

The mind is its own place, and in itself,
can make a Heaven out of Hell, a Hell of Heaven.

JOHN MILTON

In 1996, I inherited a small core group of people and began serving as lead pastor at National Community Church. We got off to a rather inauspicious start. Our first Sunday was the weekend the blizzard of '96 dumped record snowfalls on Washington DC. Only three people made it to church our first Sunday—my wife, my son, Parker, and myself. Of course, the upside is that we experienced a 633 percent growth spurt our second Sunday when nineteen people showed up.

For the first nine months, our average attendance was twenty-five people. And that included the Father, Son, and Holy Spirit on a good Sunday. I used to close my eyes in worship because it was too depressing to keep them open. I hate to even admit this, but I honestly don't think I would have attended the church if I hadn't been the pastor.

According to church demographers, more than half of all church plants never see their second year. And when I look in the rearview mirror, I can see how NCC could have easily padded that statistic. During those first few months, I didn't really feel like a pastor, and NCC didn't really feel like a church. It felt like we were thrown into the deep end, and none of us knew how to swim. We were just thrashing around trying to keep our heads above water.

Then in September of 1996 we experienced what I perceived as a huge problem. The person in charge of leasing public schools left a voicemail informing us that the DC public school we had been meeting in was being closed because of fire code violations. I wish I could say that my initial reaction was one of faith. But the truth is I had this sickening feeling in the pit of my stomach. We didn't even feel like a church yet, and we were on the verge of becoming a homeless church. I wrote these words in my journal on September 27, 1996: "I feel like we've been backed into a corner."

It honestly seemed as if we had fallen into a pit with a lion on a snowy day.

But what I saw as a daunting problem turned out to be a five-hundred-pound opportunity. We started exploring rental options on Capitol Hill, and only one door opened: the movie theaters at Union Station.

In retrospect, I can't imagine a more strategic location for a church plant. Union Station is the most visited destination in Washington DC. More than 25 million people pass through the station every year. We have our own parking garage, subway system, and bus stop. There are forty food-court restaurants right outside our theater marquee. And the station is strategically located four blocks from the Capitol and four blocks from the largest homeless shelter in the city.

God perfectly positioned us right in the middle of the marketplace, and we wouldn't want to be anywhere else. Doing church in the middle of the marketplace is part of our DNA. In fact, our long-term vision is to meet in movie theaters at metro stops throughout the DC area.

But here's the thing: It took a setback to get us where God wanted us to go. It took a God-ordained opportunity that came as a really well-disguised problem.

I'll never forget the feeling as I walked out of Union Station the day I signed the lease with the theater. Sure, I was scared. It felt like we were chasing a lion. The opportunity seemed too big for us. But I also had an overwhelming sense of destiny.

As I walked out of the station, I stopped by a kiosk and picked up *A History of Washington's Grand Terminal*. I'm a history buff, and I wanted to know a little bit more about the place where we were going to set up and have church. So I flipped open the book, and the first page was a reprint of the Bill of Congress legislating the creation of Union Station. It was signed by Theodore Roosevelt on February 28, 1903, and it said: "An act of congress to create a Union Station, and for other purposes."

The tagline—"and for other purposes"—jumped off the page and into my spirit.

More than a hundred years after that bill was signed, Union Station is serving God's purposes through the ministry of National Community Church. I don't think Theodore Roosevelt knew that he was building a pseudochurch. And Congress certainly didn't know that it was funding a church-building campaign. But I have no doubt that God knew exactly what they were building. God was setting things up for National Community Church nearly a hundred years before we even came into existence. He was working behind the scenes, engineering circumstances. And God is doing the same for you. But here's the catch: Opportunities often look like insurmountable obstacles. So, if we want to take advantage of these opportunities, we have to learn to see problems in a new way—God's way. Then our biggest problems may just start looking like our greatest opportunities.

RETHINK PRAYER

If we did an honest assessment of our prayer lives, I think we'd be amazed at the percentage of prayers aimed at *problem reduction*. Most of us pray that God would keep us out of pits with lions on snowy days. We ask God to help us steer clear of large Egyptian warriors with spears. And if we have to fight a Moabite, we ask God to make sure the numbers are stacked in our favor. But if these problems are just opportunities in disguise, our prayers are totally misdirected.

Part of me wonders if David felt a special affinity for Benaiah. David was once a bodyguard like Benaiah. And both of them were part of the exclusive lion-chasing guild. Almost like the trench effect on soldiers who face death together, there was a unique bond between David and Benaiah. They were kindred spirits. And just like Benaiah, it was a lion encounter that prepared David for his big break.

Long before becoming king, David was a simple shepherd boy. While his brothers were on the frontlines fighting the Philistines, David was stuck on the sidelines tending sheep. David felt like he had been put out to pasture, but God was honing an uncanny ability that would catapult him into the national limelight.

Right before his epic battle with Goliath, David connected the dots between his past problems and current opportunity. He reviewed his résumé so that Saul would let him fight Goliath:

"When a lion or a bear came and carried off a sheep from the flock, I went after it and struck it and rescued the sheep from its mouth. When it turned on me, I seized it by its hair and struck it and killed it. Your servant has killed both the lion and the bear; this uncircumcised Philistine will be like one of them, because he has defied the armies of the living God. The LORD who delivered me from the paw of the lion and the paw of the bear will deliver me from the hand of the Philistine."

I may be reading between the verses, but I have a hunch. I think David prayed for his sheep. I can't prove it, but I think there are some compelling reasons why he would. What child doesn't pray for his pets? I think David loved and prayed for his sheep just like we love and pray for our pets. Besides that, David's sheep were his livelihood. Just as a farmer prays for his crops, a shepherd prays for his flocks. In fact, I bet David specifically prayed that God would protect his flock by keeping lions and bears away. Makes sense, doesn't it? But David's prayers went unanswered. On numerous occasions, lions and bears attacked David's flock. I wonder if David ever questioned God: *Why doesn't God answer my prayers for safety?*

The answer dawns on David as he's getting ready to face Goliath. David puts two and two together. He sees the way his unanswered prayers actually prepared him for the opportunity of a lifetime. Every time a lion or bear attacked his flock, David had pulled a stone out of his shepherd's bag, put it in his slingshot, took aim, and fired. And David realizes that the bears and lions were target practice. They were preseason games that perfected his skills as a slingshot marksman and prepared him for his sudden-death playoff with the Giants, led by Goliath.

At the end of our lives, like David, we'll thank God for the lions and bears and giants. And like Benaiah, we'll thank God for the pits and lions and snowy days. This may sound somewhat sadistic, but follow the logic: It's our past problems that prepare us for future opportunities. So someday we may be as grateful for the bad things as the good things because the bad things helped prepare us for the good things.

At face value, landing in a pit with a lion on a snowy day is a massive problem. In fact, for most of us, it would be the last problem we ever have! But sometimes the biggest problems present the greatest opportunities for God to reveal his glory and work His purposes. No one likes being in the pits or put out to pasture, but maybe God is developing character and honing skills that will serve you later in life.

The Law of Unintended Consequences

In his *Letters to Malcolm*, C.S. Lewis said, "If God had granted all the silly prayers I've made in my life, where would I be now?" Lewis went so far as to say that someday we'll be more grateful for our prayers that *didn't* get answered than the ones that did. The reason for this is simple: Many of our prayers are misguided. We pray for comfort instead of character. We pray for an easy way out instead of the strength to make it through. We pray for no pain, when the result would be no gain. We pray that God will keep us out of pits and away from lions. But if God answered our prayer, it would rob us of our greatest opportunities. Many of our prayers would short-circuit God's plans and purposes for our lives if He answered them. Maybe we should stop asking God to get us *out* of difficult circumstances and start asking Him what He wants us to *get* out of those difficult circumstances.

Most of us blame our circumstances when things aren't going well just like we blame the ref when a game isn't going well. We look for some external scapegoat. But maybe our problem isn't our circumstances. Maybe our problem is our perspective.

Think back to chapter 2. God has a three-hundred-and-sixty-degree perspective on everything. He considers every contingency. He sees all the way around everything—every issue, every person, every experience, every problem. Most of us see a very narrow slice of reality. The best and brightest among us might have a one-degree angle of vision. It's like we are looking through a peephole. So why do we assume that what we pray for is always what's best for us? If we could see what God sees, we would pray very different prayers.

Do you remember the story of the ancient Phrygian king Midas? According to legend, Midas loved gold so much that when Dionysus granted him a wish, Midas asked that everything he touched would turn to gold. At first, Midas was delighted with his request, but when he discovered that his touch made food inedible and that his embrace made loved ones lifeless, he stumbled upon what sociologist Robert Merton called the law of unintended consequences. Like Midas, getting what we want can result in unforeseen and undesirable consequences. So much for the Midas touch.

Sometimes an unanswered prayer is God, in His sovereign wisdom, sparing us the pain of unintended consequences. Sometimes God allows what His power could prevent. Most of the time that causes us a great deal of temporal angst, but someday we will owe God as many thank-yous for the prayers He *did not* answer as the ones He did.

Maybe prayer is less about changing our circumstances than it is changing our perspective. Most of our problems aren't the byproduct of our circumstances but of our perspective on our circumstances. Maybe we need to quit praying *safe prayers*.

WORSHIP IS THE WAY OUT

In Acts 16, Paul and Silas are in stocks in a Philippian dungeon. This is not a five-star jail. It's a hell hole. Landing in an ancient middle-eastern prison isn't much better than landing in a pit with a lion on a snowy day.

A few hours earlier, Paul had cast a demon out of a fortune-teller, and her master didn't like it because his fortune-telling slave was a cash cow. So Paul and Silas were arrested.

A mob quickly formed against Paul and Silas, and the city officials ordered them stripped and beaten with wooden rods. They were severely beaten, and then they were thrown into prison. The jailer was ordered to make sure they didn't escape. So he took no chances but put them into the inner dungeon and clamped their feet in the stocks.

If I'm Paul or Silas, I'm physically, emotionally, and spiritually spent. I'm drained to the last drop. I've got nothing left to give. My back is still bleeding from the beating, and I'm in a maximum-security cell block. If I'm Paul or Silas, I'm not just ticked off at the mob. I'm slightly peeved that God didn't keep me out of this mess. After all, they were preaching the gospel.

Circumstances can't get much worse than this. And that is why Paul and Silas' reaction is so remarkable. If I had been in their place, the verse would probably read: "Around midnight, Mark was complaining about his circumstances." But not Paul and Silas.

Around midnight, Paul and Silas were praying and singing hymns to God, and the other prisoners were listening.

Let me share something I've learned from some of my personal struggles. When I get into a spiritual or emotional slump, it's usually because I've zoomed in on a problem. I'm fixating on something I don't like about myself or someone else or my circumstances. And nine times out of ten, the solution is zooming out so I can get some perspective.

So how do we zoom out? The one-word answer is *worship*.

A few years ago I had a thought that has become a worship mantra at National Community Church: Don't let what's wrong with you keep you from worshiping what's right with God.

Reframing problems is about shifting focus. You stop focusing on what's wrong with your circumstances. And you start focusing on what's right with God.

Paul and Silas could have zoomed in and complained about their circumstances. *We cast out a demon, and this is what we get? We're on a missionary journey, and we get beaten and thrown in jail? Instead of God watching our backs, our backs are bleeding from a beating!* They could have complained till the cows came home. But they made a choice to worship God in spite of their external circumstances. And that is often the most difficult and most important choice we can make.

Worship is zooming out and refocusing on the big picture. It's refocusing on the fact that two thousand years ago, Jesus died on the cross to pay the penalty for my sin. It's refocusing on the fact that God unconditionally loves me when I least expect it and least deserve it. It's refocusing on the fact that I have eternity with God to look forward to in a place where there is no mourning or sorrow or pain.

Worship is forgetting about what's wrong with you and remembering what's right with God. It is like hitting the refresh key on your computer. It restores the joy of your salvation. It recalibrates your spirit. It renews your mind. And it enables you to find something good to praise God about even when everything seems to be going wrong.

Is it easy? Absolutely not. Nothing is more difficult than praising God when nothing seems to be going right. But one of the purest forms of worship is praising God even when you don't feel like it, because it proves that your worship isn't circumstantial.

Response-Ability

Man's Search for Meaning ranks as one of the most thought-provoking books I've ever read. In it, Holocaust survivor Viktor Frankl writes about his experiences in a Nazi concentration camp.

Everything was taken away from the Jewish prisoners. They were stripped of their clothing, their pictures, and their personal belongings. The Nazi captors even took away their names and gave them numbers. Frankl was number 119,104. But Frankl said there was one thing the Nazis couldn't take away: "Everything can be taken from a man but one thing: the last of human freedoms—to choose one's attitude in any given set of circumstances."[1]

The most important choice you make every day is your attitude. Your internal attitudes are far more important than your external circumstances. Joy is *mind over matter*.

A fascinating study done by Professor Vicki Medvec reveals the relative importance of subjective attitudes over and above objective circumstances. Medvec studied Olympic medalists and discovered that bronze medalists were quantifiably happier than silver medalists. Here's why: Silver medalists tended to focus on how close they came to winning gold, so they weren't satisfied with silver; bronze medalists tended to focus on how close they came to not winning a medal at all, so they were just happy to be on the medal stand.[2]

How we feel isn't determined by objective circumstances. If that were the case, silver medalists would always be happier than bronze medalists because of objectively better results. But how we feel isn't circumstantial. It is perceptual. Our feelings are determined by our subjective focus.

Every once in a while one of our kids will get in a funk because they get focused on whatever's making them unhappy, so I pull a *Star Wars*. I'll say, "Kids, remember what Qui-gon said to Anakin: "Your focus determines your reality." At first, my kids were somewhat stupefied. But I explained to them that how they feel is a result of what they focus on.

It never ceases to amaze me how the same adversity can affect two people so differently—what poisons one person to death sweetens the other person's spirit. One person develops a critical soul and shrivels up spiritually while the other person leverages the experience as a spiritual catalyst.

When I first moved to DC after graduating from seminary, I directed a parachurch ministry called the Urban Bible Training Center. I had a Nigerian student who was in his midsixties. He could hardly talk or walk because of several strokes that affected his motor skills and speech. I still remember climbing the stairs with him. Each step was an achievement. Sometimes I would give him a ride home from class, and because his right leg was so atrophied from disuse, I had to physically lift it into the car for him. Nothing came easy.

One day I picked him up from the public housing tenement where he was living, and I'll never forget the hat he was wearing. Maybe it was the juxtaposition that struck me. He could barely walk. He could barely talk. And he was living on welfare. But he was wearing a hat that said "God is good." And he didn't just wear the hat. He walked the talk. I haven't met many people as upbeat or optimistic about life.

That moment is frozen in my memory. It was one of those moments where the Holy Spirit overshadows you in such a profound way that you'll never forget it. I actually had to choke back tears. And I remember thinking: *What right do I have to complain about anything?* Anytime I feel like throwing a pity party, I think about "the hat incident," and it helps me reframe my problems.

I think there are basically two types of people in the world: complainers and worshipers. And there isn't much circumstantial difference between the two. Complainers will always find something to complain about. Worshipers will always find something to praise

God about. They simply have different default settings.

Paul and Silas were worshipers. Their hands and feet were chained, but you can't chain the human spirit. Wouldn't you love to hear the audio track? I wish we had the MP3 of Paul and Silas singing. I don't think Paul and Silas were *NSYNC. In fact, I bet they sang off key. But they sang with a conviction that caused their fellow prisoners to listen. They praised God at the top of their voices and it set off a chain reaction. That is what worship does. It *changes* the spiritual atmosphere. It *charges* the spiritual atmosphere.

> Suddenly there was such a violent earthquake that the foundations of the prison were shaken. At once all the prison doors flew open, and everybody's chains came loose.

When you worship, it produces shock waves that register on the Richter scale. The prison doors fly open. The chains fall off. But the prisoners don't leave. In one of the most amazing conversion stories recorded in Scripture, the jailer who is about to kill himself puts his faith in Christ, and his entire family is baptized in the middle of the night. You can't script these kinds of stories! But when you worship God in the worst of circumstances, you never know what is going to happen next.

Here's a thought: The circumstances you complain about become chains that imprison you. And worship is the way out. Worship reframes our problems and refocuses our lives. It helps us get through the bad days by reminding us of how good God is.

And when you are worshipful, your eyes are more open to notice the miracles that are happening all around you all the time. One way or the other, your focus determines your reality. The *outcome* of your life will be determined by your *outlook* on life.

PROBLEM POTENTIAL

All of us want every day to be a good day. But if every day were a good day, there would be no "good" days, because there wouldn't be any bad days to compare the good days to. It's the bad days that help us appreciate the good days.

Here's what I've learned from personal experience. Sickness helps us appreciate health. Failure helps us appreciate success. Debt helps us appreciate wealth. And the tough times help us appreciate the good times. That's just the way life is. I've also learned that our worst days can become our best days.

Every year I celebrate two birthdays on two different days. I celebrate my actual birthday on November 5, but July 23 is my pseudobirthday.

In the summer of 2000, I knocked on death's door, and the lock was beginning to turn. I was experiencing severe abdominal pain. Things got progressively worse until Sunday, July 23. I tried preaching that morning, but I only got one sentence out before having to walk out of Union Station doubled over in excruciating pain.

I went to the emergency room that afternoon, but it wasn't until after midnight that an MRI revealed what was wrong. A doctor came through the curtain, and he didn't mince words. He told me my intestines had ruptured, and I needed emergency surgery immediately. While I don't remember his exact words, I'll never forget the expression on his face. I could tell my condition was life threatening.

For what it's worth, my surgeon's name was Jesus. I kid you not. I know the Hispanic version is pronounced differently than the Hebrew version, but I felt like it was God's way of saying that it was going to be all right. So I guess I'm grateful to Jesus and Jesus that I made it through the night.

I was on a respirator for two days, lost twenty-five pounds in seven days, had to endure the effects of a colostomy for six months, and have an eighteen-inch scar where a foot of intestines was removed.

Ruptured intestines would rank right up there on my list of the worst things that have ever happened to me. But I would also say it was one of the best things that ever happened to me. It is difficult to take life for granted when you've almost died. I enjoy life more because I've come to terms with my mortality. In the words of philosopher Walter Kaufman: "It makes for a better life if one has a rendezvous with death."[3] I'm certainly not prescribing near-death experiences, but what Kaufman says is true. I'm a different person because of my rendezvous with death.

July 23, 2000, could have been and should have been the date on my death certificate. And I wouldn't wish what I went through on anybody. But I've discovered that the worst days can actually turn out to be our best days if we learn the lessons God is trying to teach us. He wants us to learn to see bad experiences through the good we have gained from them.

The Adversity Effect

For most of us, landing in a pit with a lion on a snowy day would certainly qualify as bad luck. But here is what you need to see: It is adversity that gave Benaiah an opportunity to distinguish himself as a warrior. No adversity equals no opportunity. Without those extremely adverse conditions, Benaiah would have faded from the script of Scripture.

Adversity is often the seedbed of opportunity. Bad circumstances have a way of bringing the best out of us. Wild lions make valiant warriors just like rough seas make great sailors. Adversity is often a blessing in disguise.

We dream of zero gravity. We imagine what life would be like without any problems or issues or challenges. But from a biological perspective, zero gravity is hazardous to your health. Astronauts who spend any length of time in zero gravity experience serious medical complications. Without any resistance, they lose muscle mass and bone density; they experience high pulse rates and heart palpitations; and they can barely walk after reentering the earth's atmosphere.

We may dream of zero gravity, but what we really need is a healthy dose of adversity. We need some Moabites to fight and some lions to chase.

I'm sure Benaiah had scars all over his body. He was probably in the hospital as much as Evel Kneivel. But each challenge that Benaiah faced increased his capacity and fueled his confidence. Each battle prepared him for the next one. And that accumulated library of battlefield experience served him well as commander-in-chief of Israel's army.

I'm convinced that the people God uses the most are often the people who have experienced the most adversity. This isn't necessarily what I want to write, and it isn't necessarily what you want to read, but it's true. Adversity can produce an increased capacity to serve God.

Around the turn of the twentieth century, psychoanalyst Alfred Adler conducted a fascinating research project that popularized the theory of compensation. He studied art students and discovered that seventy percent of them suffered from optical anomalies. He found degenerative traces in the ears of great composers like Mozart and Beethoven. And he cited numerous examples of other people who eventually became successful in the area of their greatest weakness. Adler believed that birth defects, poverty, illnesses, and negative circumstances often prove to be the springboard of success.

What pits have you fallen into? What lions have you encountered? What giants have you faced? God wants to redeem the adversity you've experienced. He wants to recycle your adversity and turn it into a ministry.

I know so many people whose adversity has become their ministry. They go through a painful divorce or the death of a child or a destructive addiction, but God helps them climb out of the pit so they can help others in similar circumstances.

God is in the business of recycling our pain and using it for someone else's gain.

After retiring from his counseling career, influential psychiatrist Carl Jung was asked how he helped people get well. His response was profound.

> Most people came to me with an insurmountable problem. However, what happened was through our work together they discovered something more important than the problem and the problem lost its power and went away.

Now here is what you need to understand: If you don't turn your adversity into a ministry, then your pain remains your pain. But if you allow God to translate your adversity into a ministry, then your pain becomes someone else's gain.

I have a theory: The more problems you have, the more potential you have to help people.

One of the most paralyzing mistakes we make is thinking that our problems somehow disqualify us from being used by God. Let me just say it like it is: If you don't have any problems, you don't have any potential. Here's why. Your ability to help others heal is limited to where you've been wounded.

> [God] comforts us in all our troubles so that we can comfort others. When others are troubled, we will be able to give them the same comfort God has given us.

No one rolls out the red carpet and invites tragedy into their life, but our greatest gifts and passions are often the byproduct of our worst tragedies and failures. Trials have a way of helping us rediscover our purpose in life.

Remodeling

When I was a sophomore in high school, I broke my ankle playing basketball. Actually, I was just running down the court in one of our drills, and I tripped over a line on the floor. My ego hurt worse than my ankle! I spent the next month in a cast, and I remember questioning God. After all, He could have kept it from happening. But that broken ankle turned out to be a blessing in disguise.

When I broke my left ankle, I had a cast for four weeks, so I spent those four weeks hopping around on my right leg. Our high school had three floors, and it seemed like all of my classes alternated between floors that semester. So I was hopping up and down flights of stairs after every period. I was like a human pogo stick for a month.

Now, here's the thing: I had tried for years to dunk a basketball. It was my holy grail. And ironically, it took a broken ankle for me to first achieve that goal. What seemed like a setback turned into a stepping stone. I dunked my first basketball while wearing a cast on my left ankle. Here's what happened: My body simply compensated for its brokenness. When you're injured in one place, you've got to draw more strength from someplace else. My right leg grew stronger to compensate for my broken left ankle. It was the brokenness that actually increased my capacity.

In the world of strength training, it is called the principle of supercompensation. When an athlete is pushed beyond the threshold of pain and exhaustion, the body overcompensates. The more a muscle is broken down, the more it builds back up. The same is true of our bones. The two hundred and six bones in the body are constantly going through a process called remodeling. They are being broken down by osteoclasts and built back up by osteoblasts. The process of remodeling is intensified when a bone is broken. Extra osteoblasts help rebuild the bone. There is a period of weakness where the bone is more vulnerable to re-injury. That is why we wear casts. But eventually the bone ends up stronger than it was to begin with because the body overcompensates. Very rarely does a bone break in the same place twice because the bone is thicker and stronger than it was before the break.

Almost like a broken bone that needs to be reset, God breaks us where we need to be broken. He fractures the pride and lust and anger in our lives, but He does it to remodel us into His image. And once we heal, we end up stronger than we were to begin with.

It has been granted to you on behalf of Christ not only to believe on Him, but also to suffer for Him.

The word *granted* comes from the Greek root *charizomai*, which literally means "to grant a favor." This sounds ludicrous at first earshot, but it is almost as if God is saying: *Listen, I owe you a favor. Let me let you suffer.* We tend to see suffering as a necessary evil at best, but Paul calls it a divine favor. And it's not like Paul was talking theory.

Five times I received from the Jews the forty lashes minus one. Three times I was beaten with rods, once I was stoned, three times I was shipwrecked, I spent a night and a day in the open sea, I have been constantly on the move. I have been in danger from rivers, in danger from bandits, in danger from my own countrymen, in danger from Gentiles; in danger in the city, in danger in the country, in danger at sea; and in danger from false brothers.

No one had more problems than Paul. No one experienced more adversity. But God used adversity to increase his capacity. The more problems you have, the more potential you have.

I'm not suggesting that you invite adversity into your life. For all we know, Benaiah's battle with the Moabites and Egyptians was very possibly self-defense. But Benaiah recognized that those adverse circumstances could serve God's purposes. And they did. It was the way Benaiah handled the adversity that led to his military promotions. Each adverse situation was part of God's remodeling in his life. Those situations paved the way for God to remodel him as a bodyguard, army commander, and eventually commander in chief.

Where have you been broken? What adverse circumstances are you facing? Do you have any overwhelming problems?

Maybe God is remodeling you. Maybe God is increasing your capacity via adversity. Maybe the problem you never thought you could overcome will turn into a five-hundred-pound opportunity.

CHAPTER 4 REVIEW

Points to Remember

- Opportunities often look like insurmountable obstacles.
- Someday we may be as grateful for the bad things as the good things, because the bad things helped prepare us for the good things.
- We should stop asking God to *get us out* of difficult circumstances and start asking Him what He wants us *to get out of* those difficult circumstances.
- Prayer is less about changing our circumstances and more about changing our perspective.
- Worship is forgetting about what's wrong with you and remembering what's right with God.
- God wants us to learn to see bad experiences through the good we have gained from them.
- God is in the business of recycling our pain and using it for someone else's gain.

Starting Your Chase

Mark says that "the circumstances you complain about become chains that imprison you. And worship is the way out." Worship is the best way to reframe a problem. Name one area in your life where you could begin right away to replace complaining with worship.

CHAPTER 5

Guaranteed Uncertainty

To be certain of God means that we are
uncertain in all our ways; we do not know
what a day may bring forth. This is generally
said with a sigh of sadness; it should rather
be an expression of breathless expectation.

OSWALD CHAMBERS

I know one thing for sure: Benaiah didn't wake up on the morning of his lion encounter and plan out every detail. It wasn't scheduled in Outlook. It wasn't on his to-do list. I'm not even sure it was on his wish list. This lion encounter was as unplanned as a toothache.

It is so easy to read about an incident that occurred three thousand years ago and fail to appreciate the element of surprise, because we know how the story ends. We read the story and think the outcome was inevitable. Psychologists call it "hindsight bias." It is an exaggerated feeling of having been able to predict an event before it actually happened. We play the role of Monday-morning quarterback when we read Scripture. But to really appreciate the faith of Benaiah, you've got to feel what he felt *before* he killed the lion.

If you put yourself in his sandals, you'll experience a mixture of emotions. And among them is a high level of emotional uncertainty. Killing the lion was not a foregone conclusion. In fact, it was probably a statistical unlikelihood. Hand-to-hand combat with another human is one thing. Humans have tendencies. You can predict punches and counterpunches with a higher level of certainty. But savage beasts tend to be volatile and unpredictable. Their actions and reactions are less certain. Plus you have to account for topographical, physiological, and atmospheric conditions. How heavy was it snowing? Was it packing snow or slippery snow? What was the footing like in the pit? How about visibility? What time of day was it? How hungry was the lion? How well did Benaiah sleep the night before? Did he eat his Wheaties for breakfast that morning?

There are a thousand variables, and they all add up to one thing: an uncertain outcome. It could have gone either way. Heads or tails.

I'm sure Benaiah had a sense of destiny. But that sense of destiny was coupled with a degree of uncertainty. Benaiah didn't know if he'd win or lose, live or die. But he knew that God was with him.

Benaiah could have run away from the lion. And running away would have reduced uncertainty and increased security. But lion chasers are counterintuitive. They aren't afraid of venturing off the map into terra incognita. The unknown doesn't scare them. It beckons them like a long lost love or childhood dream. In a sense, security scares lion chasers more than uncertainty.

I recently had a conversation with Kurt, a friend of mine who taught information technology at one of the most respected universities in the country. The professorship had tremendous perks. And he was on the tenure track. He knew exactly what he'd be making ten years down the road. And it was good money. Guaranteed money. You would think that kind of job security would result in vocational contentment, but my friend is a lion chaser. His future was too defined, too predictable, and too safe. So Kurt decided to chase a lion. He started a dot-com business and handed in his resignation. Less than a year later, he is helping the world achieve digital bliss and leading the MP3 revolution. His leap of faith was rewarded with start-up capital to the tune of an eight-digit investment.

On one level, Kurt's decision seemed like a crazy move. He was literally running away from the financial security of a tenured professorship to chase an uncertain dot-com dream. But lion chasers are more afraid of lifelong regrets than temporary uncertainty. They don't want to get to the end of their lives and have a million what-if regrets. So they chase lions. In the short-term, it increases uncertainty. But in the long run, it reduces regrets.

I know different people have different callings. I know different people have different personalities. But I also know that embracing uncertainty is one dimension of faith. And regardless of your vocational calling or relational status, you have to do something counterintuitive if you want to reach your God-given potential and fulfill your God-given destiny. Sometimes you have to run away from security and chase uncertainty.

Isn't that what Jonathan did when he left the safety of the Israelite camp and climbed a cliff? The military stalemate was driving him crazy, so he decided to pick a fight with the Philistines. I love his modus operandi: "Perhaps the LORD will act in our behalf."

Isn't that what Abraham did when he left his family and his country to pursue the promise of God? In a day and age when the average person never traveled outside a thirty-mile radius of their birthplace, Abraham embraced uncertainty and ventured into terra incognita. "He went without knowing where he was going."

Isn't that what Noah did when he built the ark? Noah was a laughingstock for 120 years, but he embraced the uncertainty of a divine weather forecast. "Noah did everything exactly as God had commanded him."

Lion chasers challenge the status quo. They climb cliffs, move to foreign countries, and build boats in the desert. Lion chasers are often considered crazy, but they are able to do these things because they aren't afraid of uncertainty. They don't need to know what is coming next because they know that God knows. They don't need explanations for every disappointment because they know God has a plan. Lion chasers refuse to settle down because they want to experience every divine twist and turn that God has in store for them.

YOU CAN'T PLAN PENTECOST

Here is one of the biggest mistakes many of us make in our relationship with God: We focus our energies on telling God exactly *what to do, how to do it,* and *when to do it.* In fact, we repeat ourselves over and over again just to make sure God didn't miss any of the important details. But what if, instead of spending all of our energy *making plans for God,* we spent that energy *seeking God?*

Isn't that what happened on the Day of Pentecost? The disciples didn't have a plan. They were clueless. But sometimes uncertainty forces us to pray like it depends on God. And that is what the disciples did for ten days.

> When the day of Pentecost came, they were all together in one place. Suddenly a sound like the blowing of a violent wind came from heaven and filled the whole house where they were sitting. They saw what seemed to be tongues of fire that separated and came to rest on each of them. All of them were filled with the Holy Spirit and began to speak in other tongues as the Spirit enabled them.

God couldn't have scripted the Day of Pentecost any better. This outpouring of the Spirit happened during the Feast of Pentecost when Jewish pilgrims from all over the ancient world made the trek to Jerusalem. And it was those pilgrims who heard the gospel in their native tongues. Not only did three thousand believers get baptized that day, but three thousand missionaries were also commissioned to go back into every corner of the ancient world.

You couldn't coordinate an event any better than this, but here is my point: From the vantage point of the disciples, the Day of Pentecost was totally unplanned. It's not like the disciples woke up that morning thinking, *I feel like speaking in a foreign tongue today.* They had no category for what was about to happen. It was unprecedented. It's not like they made an appointment to be filled with the Holy Spirit. Peter didn't prepare a three-point sermon. And they certainly didn't pack a change of clothes for the baptism.

I'm not sure how the day started, but I'm pretty sure the disciples hit the snooze button three times before rolling out of bed, sang in the shower, put their pants on one leg at a time, brewed coffee, and read the *Jerusalem Post.*

This day started out like any other day.

There is no way they could have predicted what was about to happen. *You can't plan Pentecost.* But if you seek God for ten days in an upper room, Pentecost is bound to happen.

Here is a novel thought: What if we actually did what they did in the Bible? What if we fasted and prayed for ten days? What if we sought God with some ancient intensity instead of spending all our energy trying to eliminate His surprises? Maybe then we'd experience some ancient miracles.

One of the spiritual highlights of the past year was putting this passage into practice at National Community Church. We fasted and prayed for ten days leading up to the Day of Pentecost. It was during that Pentecost fast that I identified seven miracles that I'm believing God for. You're reading one of them. And the other six are in the process of being answered. I honestly have no idea how some of them will come to pass. One of the seven miracles I'm believing God for is that I'll experience Acts 2:41 once in my lifetime. I have no idea how or when or where it will happen, but I believe I'll be part of three thousand people getting baptized at the same time in the same place. I may be chasing that lion the rest of my life, but that is a lion worth chasing.

The Uncertainty Principle

In 1932, a German physicist named Werner Heisenberg won the Nobel Prize for his theory of quantum mechanics. Later, another of his discoveries became one of the greatest scientific revolutions of the twentieth century. For hundreds of years, determinism ruled the day. Physicists believed in a clockwork universe that was measurable and predictable. Heisenberg pulled the rug out from the under the scientific community.

Here is Heisenberg's "uncertainty principle" in a nutshell: We cannot know the precise position and momentum of a quantum particle at the same time. Here's why. Sometimes matter behaves like a particle—it appears to be in one place at one time. And sometimes matter behaves like a wave—it appears to be in several places at the same time, almost like a wave on a pond. It is the duality of nature. So here's the deal: "The imprecise measurement of initial conditions precludes the precise prediction of future outcomes." Or to put it in layman's terms: There will always be an element of uncertainty.

We had a saying in our family growing up: "You can't never always sometimes tell." I honestly don't remember where it came from or how it got started. It may be a famous aphorism for all I know. But it was our family's version of the uncertainty principle.

Life is infinitely uncertain. And you need to couple that with the fact that God is infinitely complex.

Think of God in terms of fractal geometry. Benoit Mandelbrot, the father of fractal geometry, found that some shapes, like clouds and coastlines, are infinitely complex. Any detail can be magnified to reveal even more detail ad infinitum. The technical term is "infinite complexity." Fractals are the theological equivalent of what theologians call the incomprehensibility of God. Just when we think we have God figured out, we discover a new dimension of His kaleidoscopic personality.

So if life is infinitely uncertain and God is infinitely complex, then all we can do is accept our finitude and embrace uncertainty. I think many people have the mistaken notion that faith reduces uncertainty. Nothing could be further from the truth. Faith doesn't reduce uncertainty. Faith embraces uncertainty.

We'll never have all the answers. And some people never come to terms with this truth. They feel like something is wrong with them because they can't wrap their minds around God. But maybe faith has less to do with *gaining knowledge* and more to do with *causing wonder*. Maybe a relationship with God doesn't simplify our lives. Maybe it complicates our lives in ways that they *should* be complicated.

All I know is this: Marriage complicates my life. Kids complicate my life. Pastoring a growing church complicates my life. Wealth will complicate your taxes, and success will complicate your schedule. Thank God for complications!

The last time I checked the parable of the talents, the reward for good work wasn't an early retirement or extended vacation. The reward for good work was more work. Complications are often a byproduct of blessing.

A relationship with God will complicate your life, but it will complicate your life in ways it *should* be complicated. Sin will complicate your life in ways that it *shouldn't* be complicated. One way or the other, life is complicated. Good complications or bad complications—it's your choice.

Are We There Yet?

The longer I live, the more I think that spiritual maturity is less about figuring out the future and more about a moment-by-moment sensitivity to the Spirit of God. I'm not saying we shouldn't make plans. But you might want to use a pencil with an eraser and have a shredder handy.

I have a tangible reminder of how pointless the best-laid plans of mice and men can be. I have an inch-thick document in one of my files. It is *my* twenty-five-year plan for our failed church plant when I was in graduate school. We never even had our first service, but I had the next 1,300 Sundays all planned out. What a joke. Seriously! Can't you just hear God chuckling as I was busy planning? If you want to give God a good laugh, give Him a detailed description of where you'll be and what you'll be doing twenty-five years from now.

Most of you never would have guessed ten years ago that you'd be doing what you're doing or living where you're living. And while you may have plans for the future, you have no idea what life will look like ten years from now. But that's okay. I just don't think spiritual maturity results in higher degrees of predictability.

It's not like Benaiah had a twenty-five-year occupational strategy in place.

Step one: Kill a lion in a pit on a snowy day.
Step two: Apply for a job as bodyguard for the King of Israel.
Step three: Work my way up the ranks until I become commander in chief of Israel's army.

That isn't how life works.

I believe in planning. I believe in goal setting. But there are some things in life you can't plan or predict. And that drives the obsessive-compulsive part of us crazy. We want control, but the decision to follow Christ is a relinquishment of control. Following Christ is letting Jesus take the wheel. Of course, some of us act like backseat drivers. Or worse yet, we're like little kids that make their parents crazy by asking one question over and over again: *Are we there yet?*

I honestly think that question reveals something genetically wired into the human psyche. It comes standard. And while we may stop pestering our parents, we never outgrow the desire to know exactly where we're headed and exactly when we'll get there. We want a complete itinerary with everything mapped out.

What I'm trying to say in a nice way is this: We're control freaks. But faith involves a loss of control. And with the loss of control comes the loss of certainty. You never know when a five-hundred-pound lion may cross your path. And faith is the willingness and readiness to embrace those uncertainties.

Puppet God

Most of us have a love/hate relationship with uncertainty. We hate *negative uncertainties*—the bad things that happen that we didn't expect to happen. We don't like pink slips, IRS audits, or flat tires. No fun. But we love *positive uncertainties*—the good things that happen that we didn't expect. Flowers for no reason. An unsolicited bear hug from your kids. A surprise birthday party. But here's the thing: You can't have it both ways.

There is part of us that wants a puppet God. We want to pull the strings like a puppeteer, but even God doesn't treat us like puppets. Part of us wants a manageable God, but if God was manageable, we'd be miserable. Can you imagine a world where everything that happened was predictable? How boring would that be? A world without uncertainty would be a world without butterflies in your stomach or come-from-behind upsets.

I used to hate uncertainty, but I'm learning to love it. It is an acquired taste. I am discovering that the greatest moments in life are unscripted. They are unrehearsed and unplanned and unpredictable, and that is precisely what makes them unforgettable.

A couple months ago we were on vacation in Orlando, Florida. One morning we were sitting at a stoplight in our rental van. The light turned green, and the car in front of us didn't go, so I decided to give them a little "love tap" on the horn. But when I hit the horn, it got jammed, and I couldn't turn it off. The poor people in front of us! They must have thought I was a raging lunatic!

I quickly pulled into a gas station while everybody stared at us. We were mortified, but fortunately the horn stopped honking when I turned the van off. So I started the van back up, and we got onto the highway. About two miles down the road, the horn started honking again without me even touching it. Scout's honor. So we were driving down the highway at seventy miles per hour blaring our horn at everybody and their brother. I'm not sure what people were thinking, but it felt like we were screaming at people. *Get out of my lane, sucker! This road belongs to us!*

I honestly didn't know what to do. Malfunctioning horns weren't covered in my driver's ed class. So I did what I do whenever anything is broken: I hit it. I just kept pounding the horn, and it would actually stop honking for a few seconds. Then it would sporadically start honking again.

That fifteen-minute ride would rank as one of the most chaotic driving experiences of my adult life. But you know what? We're still laughing about it months later. In fact, I don't think my kids will ever forget the now infamous "honking horn" incident.

Most of our trip was preplanned. We planned on swimming. We planned on catching lizards. We planned on visiting the Magic

Kingdom. And all of those planned activities were a blast. But the highlight of the trip was totally unplanned. You can't plan a horn malfunction. But that horn malfunction caused as much laughter as the rest of the trip combined.

Now here's my point: Some of the best things in life are totally unplanned and unscripted.

I'm no movie critic, but in my humble entertainment estimation, the greatest movies have the highest levels of uncertainty. Whether the uncertainty is romantic or dramatic, scripts with the highest level of uncertainty make the best movies. In the same vein, I think high levels of uncertainty make the best lives.

You wouldn't be reading a book about a bodyguard named Benaiah if it weren't for the high levels of uncertainty he experienced. If Benaiah had managed to avoid the uncertain circumstances recorded in Scripture, he would have never made the canonical cut. Benaiah would have been edited out of The Script.

Faith is embracing the uncertainties of life. It is chasing the lions that cross our paths. It is recognizing a divine appointment when you see one.

Embrace relational uncertainty. It's called *romance*. Embrace spiritual uncertainty. It's called *mystery*. Embrace occupational uncertainty. It's called *destiny*. Embrace emotional uncertainty. It's called *joy*. Embrace intellectual uncertainty. It's called *revelation*.

The Great Banana Peel

I cannot promise that being a Christ follower will reduce uncertainty in your life. In fact, we have a core value at National Community Church: Expect the unexpected. That value is based on the fact that Jesus was and is predictably unpredictable. Have you read the Gospels lately? More than half the time, Jesus says and does the opposite of what the disciples expect. There is never a dull moment when you are following in the footsteps of Christ. You never know who you'll meet, what you'll do, or where you'll go. Seriously, do you think these simple fishermen ever thought they would meet kings, travel to the four corners of the ancient world, and turn the world upside down? No way! But when you follow Jesus, all bets are off. Anything can happen. And that is what makes the adventure so uncertain—and so exciting.

Jesus never promised security. What he promised was uncertainty:

"Foxes have holes and birds of the air have nests, but the Son of Man has no place to lay his head."

I'm not convinced that following Christ reduces *circumstantial* uncertainty. I think it reduces *spiritual* uncertainty. I think we can have what Scripture describes as "a peace that passes understanding." I think we can *know that we know* that we are children of God, our sins are forgiven, and we're going to spend eternity in heaven. But following Christ may actually increase uncertainty in other areas of our lives.

When you follow Christ, it is sort of like tracking a fox or chasing a bird: You never know where it's going to take you. Jesus didn't even know where he would end up at the end of every day. His disciples learned to embrace the daily uncertainty that was part and parcel of following Christ.

I know that part of us wants God to take us to a three act play with a clearly defined plot that has a beginning, a middle, and an end. But Jesus takes us to the Improv instead. We want the entire script up front, but that would undermine our dependence upon the Holy Spirit. Following Jesus and keeping in step with the Spirit require the art of improvisation. We've got to develop an affinity for uncertainty and learn to enjoy the journey.

I love the way Robert Fulghum describes uncertainty in his book

From Beginning to End.[1] Fulghum shares the speech he gives to the bride and groom right before the wedding ceremony. They have planned the wedding right down to the last detail. They want everything to go perfectly as planned. But Fulghum reminds them of a simple truth: "Weddings are a lot like any other occasion in life. Anything can happen. The great banana peel of existence is always on the floor somewhere."

Sometimes things go terribly wrong. They did at the wedding in Cana. Running out of wine probably resulted in the first marital spat between bride and groom. *I thought you ordered the wine, sweetie? No, I told you to get it, honey!* But that mishap set the stage for Jesus' first miracle, didn't it? If everything had gone according to plan, Jesus would have never changed the molecular structure of water and turned it into wine. *No problem equals no miracle.*

Now let me flip the coin. Robert Fulghum acknowledges that anything might go wrong. But he also says that anything might go right. "Sometimes the unexpected is an unforgettable moment that transforms a standard wedding into a memorable experience. The sweetest memories are seldom the result of planning."

I have officiated a lot of weddings, and my favorite moments are almost always unscripted. I love it when the bride and groom experience what I would call unrehearsed emotion during their vows. I love it when the crazy uncle does his crazy dance at the reception. We all have one, don't we? I love flower girls and ring bearers. The best age is right around three years old. No amount of rehearsing can remove the element of uncertainty as they walk down the center aisle. And please forgive me for this, but I love it when someone faints in a wedding. I certainly don't want anybody to get injured, but that adds so much to a ceremony!

I was in a friend's wedding several years ago, and the bridesmaid I was paired up with fainted. It was surreal. I remember standing there and experiencing it like it was happening in slow motion. It was a *Matrix* moment. All these thoughts flooded my mind as she was falling. *I've never seen anyone faint. I wonder if it hurts when you hit the ground. I wonder what the bride and groom will think.* Of course, the one thought that didn't cross my mind was: *Maybe I should catch her.* I just watched her fall like a felled tree!

We naturally want everything to go according to plan, but the element of surprise infuses life with so much joy. Thank God for uncertainty and unpredictability. The alternative is monotony.

EXPLANATORY STYLE

At the end of the day, embracing uncertainty comes back to our perspective on life. (Doesn't everything?) Do we really believe that God is ordering every footstep even when it feels like we've taken a misstep? Do we really believe that God is sovereign when nothing seems to be going our way? Do we really believe that God is good even when bad things happen to us?

It is the sovereignty of God that gives us a sense of destiny. And it is the sense of destiny that helps us embrace the positive and negative uncertainties that happen in our lives.

In his book *Learned Optimism*, Dr. Martin Seligman says that all of us have what he calls an "explanatory style" to account for life's experiences: "Explanatory style is the manner in which you habitually explain to yourself why events happen."[2]

Let me extrapolate.

You're at a restaurant waiting for your date. You were supposed to meet at seven o'clock sharp, but forty-five minutes later your date is a no-show. At some point you need to explain to yourself why. You might think to yourself, *He stood me up,* causing you to become mad. Or you might jump to conclusions—*She doesn't love me anymore*—causing you to become sad. You could think, *He was in an accident,* causing you to feel anxious. You might think, *She's working overtime so that she can pay for our meal,* causing you to feel grateful. (Naïve, but grateful.) You might think, *She's with another man,* causing you to feel jealous. Or you might think, *This gives me a perfect excuse to break up with him,* causing you to feel relieved.

Same situation. Very different explanations.

There are lots of different explanations for every experience. And while you can't control your experiences, you can control your explanations. And the truth is this: your explanations are more important than your experiences. In the words of Dr. Seligman: "Your way of explaining events to yourself determines how helpless you become, or how energized, when you encounter everyday setbacks as well as momentous defeats."[3]

One of the most tragic storylines in Scripture is found in the book of Genesis. When Joseph was a teenager, his brothers faked his death and sold him into slavery. That would cause enough psychopathology to last a lifetime for most people, but it was only the tip of the pyramid for Joseph. When Joseph resisted the sexual advances of Potiphar's wife, he was unjustly thrown into an Egyptian dungeon on attempted rape charges. For thirteen years things went from bad to worse. But Joseph never lost faith because his faith wasn't contingent upon his circumstances. After thirteen years of what seemed like bad luck, in what must be the most precipitous rise to power in political history, Joseph interpreted a dream and went from prisoner to prime minister of Egypt.

Joseph could have come up with any number of explanations for his experiences when things weren't going his way. *God has forsaken me. God is angry with me. God has forgotten me. God has given up on me.* But Joseph's explanation is Genesis 50:20. Joseph looks in the rearview mirror and reflects on all the dysfunction, all the injustice, all the betrayal, and all the pain. And he says to his brothers, the same brothers who faked his death and sold him into slavery:

> You intended to harm me, but God intended it for good
> to accomplish what is now being done, the saving of many
> lives.

This one verse summarizes Joseph's outlook on life and reveals his explanatory style. Joseph was able to see the purposes of God in his past experiences. Genesis 50:20 is the lens through which each of us must view our past, present, and future. Everyone's path is littered with the debris of dysfunction and disappointment. We've all been misjudged or misled. And we will be many more times before our lives are over. But God is in the business of using those experiences to prepare us for future opportunities.

Unanswered Questions

Not long ago, my daughter Summer asked a question out of nowhere: "Dad, why did God create mosquitoes?" That's a tough question. I made up some lame answer like, "Lizards eat them." But to be perfectly honest, I'm not sure why God made mosquitoes. I don't like them. I don't lose sleep over it, but I think it's one of those unanswerable questions. By the way, Summer also said, "I've been saving that question for God for two years."

We all have questions we've been saving for God, don't we?

And most of them aren't as benign as "Why did God make mosquitoes?" We have malignant questions that metastasize. *How could God let my spouse leave me like that? Why is my child the one in ten thousand with a rare genetic disorder? Why didn't someone do something to stop the abuse?*

Positive uncertainties produce some of the most joyful moments in life, but I don't want to make light of the negative uncertainties.

They are painful and stressful.

Maybe you're facing the relational uncertainty called divorce. Maybe downsizing at work is causing some occupational uncertainty. Or maybe you've got lots of unanswered questions that are causing spiritual uncertainty.

Someday God will answer all of our malignant questions. Someday God will explain all our painful experiences. Someday God will resolve all our spiritual paradoxes. In the meantime, I have a Deuteronomy 29:29 file filled with things I don't understand.

There are secrets the Lord God has not revealed to us.

At some point in our spiritual journeys, we run into something called reality. And it usually happens when we're driving sixty miles per hour with no seat belt on! The result is spiritual whiplash. Simple answers don't suffice, and God doesn't fit into the nice, neat boxes He used to fit into. The psychological term for this experience is "cognitive dissonance." We experience psychological conflict resulting from incongruous beliefs. In other words, something happens that doesn't jibe with what we believe.

Dissonance comes in two primary flavors: unanswerable questions and unexplainable experiences. And I have tasted lots of both flavors.

One of my unanswered questions is why my father-in-law, Bob, passed away in the prime of his life. Not only did we lose a dad, but I also lost my mentor in ministry. I wouldn't be doing what I'm doing if it weren't for his influence in my life. Bob planted and then pastored Calvary Church in Naperville, Illinois, for more than thirty years. And God used him in a profound way to impact tens of thousands of lives.

In January of 1998, Bob went in for a routine physical. The doctor didn't just give him a clean bill of health; he literally said you could drive a Mack truck through his arteries. One week later he died of a heart attack. And I remember two distinct feelings. I remember feeling *helpless*. There was nothing I could do to bring him back. And I remember feeling *overwhelmed*. You almost go into a state of shock because you experience emotional overload. The grief is consuming. If you've lost a loved one, you know the feeling. During the funeral, I realized that I couldn't stop sighing. I later read that sighing is one way we process grief. It is a physiological response to distress. I didn't know how to vent or verbalize what I was feeling, so I sighed.

It was during that time that I discovered what is now one of my favorite Psalms:

Give ear to my words, O Lord, consider my sighing.

That little phrase—"consider my sighing"—became a source of strength for me. I didn't know how to pray or what to say, but I knew God was considering my sighing. Even when we can't put our frustration or anger or doubt or discouragement or grief into words, God hears and translates those low-frequency distress signals we call sighs.

Maybe prayer is much more than a combination of the twenty-six letters of the English alphabet into words? I love Ted Loder's perspective in *Guerillas of Grace*:

How shall I pray?
Are tears prayers, Lord?
Are screams prayers,
    or groans
        or sighs
            or curses?
Can trembling hands be lifted to you,

or clenched fists
> or the cold sweat that trickles down my back
>> or the cramps that knot my stomach?
Will you accept my prayers, Lord,
> my real prayers,
>> rooted in the muck and mud and rock of my life,
and not just the pretty, cut-flower, gracefully arranged
bouquet of words?
Will you accept me, Lord,
> as I really am,
>> messed up mixture of glory and grime?[4]

Sometimes it feels like God isn't listening, but He considers every sigh. Not only that, He is interceding for us day and night. Scripture says that God makes prayers out of our wordless sighs and aching groans.

The Holy Spirit helps us in our distress. For we don't even know what we should pray for, nor how we should pray. But the Holy Spirit prays for us with groanings that cannot be expressed in words.

Here is an incredible thought: Long before you woke up this morning the Holy Spirit was interceding for you. And long after you go to bed tonight, the Holy Spirit will still be interceding for you. That ought to change the way we wake up and fall asleep. That ought to give us the courage to chase lions.

Connect the Dots

The greatest hazard to your spiritual health is thinking that your past is haphazard or that your future is left up to chance alone. It is anything but. I can't promise that everything will make sense on the near side of eternity, but that shouldn't shake our confidence, because our confidence isn't contingent upon our circumstances. Our confidence is contingent upon the character of God. Our circumstances may not make sense, but we know that God is planning His work and working His plan.

When I was five years old, our family went to see a movie called *The Hiding Place*. The movie documented the story of a woman named Corrie ten Boom who miraculously survived the Nazi concentration camps. It was after watching that movie that I took my first step of faith. As my mom tucked me into bed that night, I asked her if I could ask Jesus into my heart.

I have often wondered if Corrie questioned God. She must have. Her family was hiding Jews. *Why would God allow them to be captured?* Her father and sister died in the camps. *How could God let that happen?*

Corrie used to speak to audiences about her horrific experiences in the concentration camps, and she would often look down while she talked. She wasn't reading her notes. She was actually working on a piece of needlepoint. After sharing about the doubt and anger and pain she experienced, Corrie would reveal the needlepoint. She would hold up the backside of the needlepoint to reveal a jumble of colors and threads with no discernible pattern. And she'd say, "This is how we see our lives." Then she would turn the needlepoint over to reveal the design on the other side, and Corrie would conclude by saying: "This is how God views your life, and someday we will have the privilege of viewing it from His point of view."

Corrie could have questioned why she had to suffer in Nazi concentration camps. It didn't make sense. It was unfair. But what I do know is this: Somehow God used the suffering of a woman named Corrie ten Boom living in Holland in 1944 to lead a five-year-old boy named Mark Batterson living in Minneapolis, Minnesota, to Christ more than thirty years later. I'm the beneficiary of Corrie ten Boom's unanswerable questions and unexplainable experiences.

Some of your experiences won't make sense this side of eternity, but lion chasers know that God is connecting the dots in ways they can't comprehend. Lion chasers are humble enough to let God call the shots and brave enough to follow where He leads.

Chapter 5 Review

Points to Remember

- You have to do something counterintuitive if you want to reach your God-given potential and fulfill your God-given destiny.
- Stop spending all your energy *making plans* for God, and start *seeking* God.
- Faith is embracing uncertainty.
- Following Christ reduces *spiritual* uncertainty, but it doesn't reduce *circumstantial* uncertainty.
- Your explanations are more important than your experiences. While you can't control your experiences, you can control your explanations.
- Some of your experiences won't make sense this side of eternity, but lion chasers know that God is connecting the dots in ways they can't comprehend.

Starting Your Chase

What questions do you have for God in your own Deuteronomy 29:29 ("There are secrets the Lord God has not revealed to us") file? What could you do to help yourself accept that they may not get answered in your lifetime?

CHAPTER 6

Playing It Safe Is Risky

*Twenty years from now you will be more
disappointed by the things you didn't do than
by the ones you did do. So throw off the bowlines.
Sail away from the safe harbor.
Catch the trade winds in your sails.
Explore. Dream. Discover.*

MARK TWAIN

I have a friend, Lee, who pastors one of the fastest-growing churches in America. Lee doesn't look like your typical pastor. He doesn't dress like your typical pastor. And he had no formal training for ministry. But I know of few people who are being used by God like my "unqualified" and "inexperienced" friend. And it all started with a calculated risk that he took about ten years ago.

Lee was on the executive track at Microsoft, making well into the six digits, but even more significantly, he had accumulated sixteen thousand share options valued at several million dollars. And that is when he started sensing God calling him to plant a church. I'm sure my friend could have come up with several million excuses not to pursue church planting. His boss actually offered him a promotion and an even fatter paycheck if he would stay at Microsoft. But my friend quit his job and took a church-planting position paying $26,000. Not only did he take a pay cut, he also forfeited his stock options.

Now here is what rocked my world. When Lee gave up his sixteen thousand share options, he made one request of God: "Give me one soul for every share of stock I'm giving up." God is well on His way to answering that prayer. At last count the church he serves as pastor is averaging more than six thousand people in weekly attendance.

So why is God using Lee in such a profound way? I think God is using him for the same reason He used Benaiah or Nehemiah or Abraham. Scan the pages of Scripture and you'll find that God uses risk-takers. Benaiah risked his life chasing the lion. Nehemiah risked his position in the Babylonian administration to rebuild the wall of Jerusalem. And Abraham risked losing his son.

The circumstances vary, but the law of risk is universal and eternal: The more you're willing to risk, the more God can use you. And if you're willing to risk *everything*, then there is *nothing* God can't do in you and through you.

Lee took a multimillion-dollar risk. But that calculated risk is paying eternal dividends. I recently watched one of his church's baptism videos, and it showed hundreds of people publicly declaring their faith in Christ. Think about how those hundreds of people will influence their relational networks. Think of the generational blessing that will be passed down from parents to children. And it all traces back to one calculated risk. My friend had the guts to chase a lion.

Almost like Dr. Jekyll and Mr. Hyde, we are part coward and part daredevil. The coward is constantly whispering, *Better safe than sorry.* The daredevil is whispering, *Nothing ventured, nothing gained.*

Which voice are you going to listen to?

What are you going to do when you cross paths with a lion? Are you going to run away from risk like a scaredy-cat? Or are you going to run after it like a lion chaser? That decision will determine your ultimate destiny.

The Butterfly Effect

In 1960, an MIT meteorologist named Edward Lorenz made an accidental discovery while he was trying to develop a computer program that could simulate and forecast weather conditions. One day he was in a hurry, and instead of entering .506127, the number he had used in an earlier trial, he rounded to the nearest thousandth, or .506. Lorenz figured that rounding the number to the nearest thousandth would be inconsequential. He left the lab, and when he returned he found a radical change in the weather conditions. Lorenz estimated that the numerical difference between the original number and the rounded number was the equivalent of a puff of wind created by a butterfly's wing. He concluded that a minor event like the flapping of a butterfly's wing could conceivably alter wind currents sufficiently to eventually change weather conditions thousands of miles away. Lorenz then introduced the scientific community to "the butterfly effect."

In his book *Chaos*, James Gleick defines the butterfly effect this way: "Tiny differences in input [can] quickly become overwhelming differences in output."[1]

It's true in science. It's true in life. Small changes and small choices become magnified over time and have major consequences. Everything we change changes everything. Too often we fail to connect the dots between choices and consequences. Every choice has a domino effect that can alter our destiny.

According to Scripture, Benaiah climbed all the way up the military chain of command to become commander in chief of Israel's army. But his rank is really the byproduct of three calculated risks he took decades before. 2 Samuel 23 records three dominos: Benaiah took on two Moabites despite being outnumbered; he chased a lion despite snowy conditions; and he fought an Egyptian despite the fact that he was out-armed.

What if Benaiah had decided that there were *too many* Moabites to make it a fair fight? What if Benaiah had decided it was *too dangerous* to chase a five-hundred-pound lion? What if he had decided that the seven-and-a-half-foot-tall Egyptian was *too big*?

I think it's safe to say that Benaiah would have never become commander of David's bodyguard, let alone commander in chief of Israel's army.

It was Benaiah's willingness to risk life and limb that set him apart. Scripture says that Benaiah was "more honored than the other members of the Thirty [an elite group among David's fighting men]."

Lion chasers are risk takers. They have learned that playing it safe is risky. They recognize that the best you can do if you run away from a lion is break even. You might save your skin, but you won't have a lion skin hanging on your wall either. No risk equals no reward.

As I reflect on my own life, I realize that most of the good things that have happened are the byproduct of a few calculated risks. My wife and my kids are the result of risk. So is our home, our life in DC, our church. Becoming a multisite church and launching our second location was a risk. Opening a coffeehouse was a risk. Every move was scary, uncertain, and usually seemed pretty crazy.

But I can't imagine what my life would look like if I had run away from risk. The genealogy of blessing always traces back to God-ordained risks. All the good things I've experienced in my marriage, my life, and my ministry are the byproduct of the risks I have taken. And the bigger the risk, the bigger the reward.

The Tipping Point

Life is full of what I call "one small step, one giant leap" moments. These are the experiences that forever change the trajectory of our lives; these are the moments that couldn't be planned or predicted; these are the decisions that divide our lives into chapters.

At the beginning of my spiritual journey, I would have considered myself a Christ follower, but if the truth be told, it was less about me following Christ and more about Christ following me. Up until I was nineteen years old, I wasn't really serving God's purposes. I was asking God to serve my purposes. My intentions were good, but I wasn't revolving my life around God. I wanted God to revolve Himself around me. But that changed at the end of my freshman year at the University of Chicago when I asked God a dangerous question: "What do you want me to do with my life?" (By the way, the only thing more dangerous than *asking* that question is *not asking* that question.)

In typical God fashion, I didn't get an answer right away. No writing on the wall. I experienced high levels of stress, sort of like the tension you feel when you're driving through fog. I had a hard time relaxing that summer. It felt like I was in no man's land. But I began to seek God with intensity and intentionality. And in retrospect, I'm grateful that it was as long and as hard as it was to discover my calling, because easy answers produce shallow convictions.

The compass needle stopped spinning, and I found true north in August of 1989. Our family was vacationing at Lake Ida in rural Alexandria, Minnesota. I got up around sunrise to take a prayer walk. I walked down some deserted dirt roads and took a shortcut through a cow pasture. Right in the middle of that cow pasture I heard what I would describe as the inaudible yet unmistakable voice of God. Full-time ministry wasn't even on my radar a year before, but I knew that God was calling me to plant and pastor a church. I had no idea what steps to take or where the road would lead, but I knew I had to take a calculated risk. So I made a pretty radical decision. I decided to transfer from the University of Chicago to Central Bible College in Springfield, Missouri.

Most of my friends thought I was crazy. People told me I was committing academic suicide. The U of C was the third-ranked university in the country that year by *U.S. News & World Report*. CBC wasn't even regionally accredited at that point. And I had to give up my shooting-guard spot on the basketball team and a full-ride academic scholarship. The decision to transfer schools made no sense academically, financially, or athletically. Transferring schools seemed about as logical as chasing a lion, but most God-ordained dreams die because we aren't willing to do something that seems illogical.

I can honestly say that I wouldn't want to be anyplace else doing anything else at this stage in my life. I'm living my dream as lead pastor of National Community Church. And I realize that all the joy and fulfillment I have experienced over the past decade traces back to one small step that proved to be one giant leap. There is no way I would have been ready to pastor a church plant when I was twenty-six if it weren't for my two and a half years at Central Bible College.

Good *is* often the enemy of great. On paper, I had a good situation at the University of Chicago, but good isn't good enough. Sometimes taking a calculated risk means giving up something that is good so you can experience something that is great. In a sense, sin is short-changing ourselves and short-changing God. It is settling for anything less than God's best. Faith is the exact opposite. Faith is renouncing lesser goods for something greater. And it always involves a calculated risk.

I'm convinced that the only thing between you and your destiny is one small act of courage. One courageous choice may be the only thing between you and your dream becoming reality. And it may be as simple as placing a phone call, downloading an application, or sending an e-mail. But you've got to push over the first domino.

I'm neither a historian nor the son of a historian, but let me make an observation: It is small acts of courage that change the course of history. Someone takes a risk or takes a stand. Someone makes a courageous decision or courageous sacrifice. And it has a domino effect.

Esther says, "If I perish, I perish." A Jewish cupbearer named Nehemiah says, "If it pleases the king and if your servant has found favor in his sight, let him send me to the city in Judah where my fathers are buried so that I can rebuild it." Three Jewish friends refuse to bow down to a Babylonian idol: "We do not need to defend ourselves before you in this matter. If we are thrown into the blazing furnace, the God we serve is able to save us from it." Two disciples named Peter and John say, "We cannot help speaking about what we have seen and heard."

Those courageous decisions proved to be tipping points.

Esther saved the Jewish remnant from genocide. Nehemiah rebuilt the wall of Jerusalem. The three amigos were promoted to positions of political power in Babylon. And the entire ancient world heard the gospel because Peter and John couldn't and wouldn't be silenced.

For Benaiah, the tipping point was chasing a lion into a pit on a snowy day and killing it. The normal reaction by the normal person, when encountering a man-eating lion in the wild, would have been to adopt a defensive posture. Benaiah could have run away, and no one would have blamed him. Benaiah could have run away, and no one would have thought any less of him. He could have played it safe, and no one would have considered him a coward. But Benaiah made a split-second decision. He took one small step toward the lion, and it proved to be one giant leap toward his ultimate destiny as commander in chief of Israel's army.

This had to be the longest and hardest step in his life. It was illogical. It was counterintuitive. It was scary. But Benaiah didn't take a step back. He took a step forward. He didn't run away from the lion. He ran toward it kamikaze style.

And that one small step in the direction of the lion proved to be a tipping point in his life.

Risky Business

There is nothing easy about taking risks. Even seemingly small risks can be as scary as chasing a lion or hand-to-hand combat with a giant Egyptian. But lion chasers have the courage to overcome inaction inertia. Their fear of *missing out* is greater than their fear of *messing up*.

A few years ago I got an e-mail from a lion chaser named Natalie. She was faced with a tough decision, and I served as a sounding board:

> About a month ago I applied for a position in Harvard's WorldTeach Program. I knew it was a long shot, but there were too many "coincidences" for me to ignore the opportunity God was placing before me. Last week you talked about stepping out in faith to follow God's call. You said, "God is always calling us into terra incognita. He wants us to go where we've never gone and do what we've never done."
>
> In a nutshell, the government of the Marshall Islands has named educational reform as their top priority. I have been asked to be one of the thirty American delegates to help. Am I scared to go to a country that has electricity on only one of its 1,229 islands? That is "connected" not through Internet or cell phones, but by short-wave radio? That is a six-plus hour flight from any other major civilization? That has the highest incidence of radiation poisoning anywhere on earth? To answer these and the other questions swirling in my head, I would say, "Yes." Have I thought about turning down the

offer? Yes. Do I believe that turning down the offer would be refusing God's call? Yes. Will I go? Yes."

Obedience is a willingness to do whatever, whenever, wherever God calls us. And that looks very different for each of us. It doesn't always necessitate going halfway around the world. Often the most courageous actions only require us going across the room or across the street.

I'm not sure what lion God has called you to chase. It may mean teaching at an inner-city school or starting a business or becoming a foster parent. It may mean applying to a graduate program or resigning a position. It may mean ending a relationship or beginning a new one. But one thing is for sure: You can't remove risk from the equation.

Part of me wonders if we've been sold a bill of goods. Is it just me or does it seem like some people act as if faith is the reduction of risk? They act as if the goal of faith is to eliminate risk so our lives are, in the words of the old hymn, "safe and secure from all alarm."

Have you read the Bible lately? Faith is risky business.

The goal of faith is *not* the elimination of risk. In fact, the greatest risk is taking no risks. Isn't that the principle in the parable of the talents? Jesus commends the two men who take a risk and make a return. But the servant who buries his talent and breaks even is called "wicked." Why? Because he wasn't willing to take a calculated risk. Maybe risk taking is at the heart of righteousness. Maybe righteousness has less to do with *not doing anything wrong* and more to do with *doing things right*. Righteousness is using our God-given gifts to their God-given potential. And that requires risk. Maybe our view of sanctification is too sanitized. Maybe our view of Christianity is too civilized. Maybe we need to reconsider what made our spiritual ancestors heroic.

Some faced jeers and flogging, while still others were chained and put in prison. They were stoned; they were sawed in two; they were put to death by the sword. They went about in sheepskins and goatskins, destitute, persecuted and mistreated—the world was not worthy of them. They wandered in deserts and mountains, and in caves and holes in the ground.

God never promised us a risk-free existence. Bad things happen to good people. And good things happen to bad people. And that causes tremendous angst unless we look at life through the eyes of eternity. The risks taken by many heroes of the faith ended in dismemberment and death. Not exactly a storybook ending. God never promised that the reward for risk would always be given this side of eternity. But He does promise that every God-ordained risk will be rewarded on the flipside of the space-time continuum.

No Sacrifice

I think many people make a fundamental mistake in the way they view their relationship with God. They view it in win/lose terms. They see it as a zero-sum game. They focus on what they have to *give up* and fail to realize how much more they *get back*. A relationship with God is the ultimate win/win relationship.

Let me go out on a theological limb: I don't think there is any such thing as sacrifice when you're a follower of Christ.

Sure, we are called to "deny ourselves" and "take up our cross." We're called to "lose our lives so that we can find them." And we certainly experience temporary loss. But I don't think anyone has ever sacrificed anything for God. Why? Because we always get back more than we give up. And if you get back more than you gave up, have you really sacrificed anything at all?

On December 4, 1857, the famous missionary David Livingstone gave a speech at Cambridge University.

People talk of the sacrifice I have made in spending so much of my life in Africa.... Away with the word in such a view and with such a thought! It is emphatically no sacrifice. Say rather it is a privilege. Anxiety, sickness, suffering, or danger now and then with a foregoing of the common conveniences and charities of this life may make us pause and cause the spirit to waver and the soul to sink; but let this only be for a moment. All these are nothing when compared with the glory which shall be revealed in and for us. I never made a sacrifice.

You've never sacrificed anything for God. But let me push the envelope even further: If you were to always act in your greatest self-interest, you would *always* obey God. That is what I mean by a win/win relationship.

"I tell you the truth, at the renewal of all things, when the Son of Man sits on his glorious throne, you who have followed me will also sit on twelve thrones, judging the twelve tribes of Israel. And everyone who has left houses or brothers or sisters or father or mother or children or fields for my sake will receive a hundred times as much and will inherit eternal life."

There is an old aphorism: "No one ever bet too much on a winning horse." I know this for sure: The only regrets we'll have at the end of our lives will be that we didn't seek God more or seek God sooner. That's it.

Playing it Safe is Risky

We have a core value at NCC: Playing it safe is risky. And that core value is epitomized in Matthew 14. In a sense, Matthew 14 is one of those passages of Scripture that double as a microcosm of life.

The disciples were rowing across the Sea of Galilee in the middle of the night, and Jesus walked out to them on the water. At first, the disciples thought he was a ghost. In fact, Scripture says these manly fishermen screamed like frightened children. I honestly think this passage reveals the prankster in Jesus. Have you ever hid around a corner and scared the living daylights out of someone? Jesus took it to a new level. But he had an unfair advantage when it came to pulling pranks: He could walk on water.

Once the disciples stopped screaming and Jesus stopped chuckling, he said, "Don't be afraid." Peter said, "Lord, if it's really you, tell me to come to you by walking on the water." And Jesus said, "Come." So Peter takes one small step out of the boat and one giant leap toward Jesus. And he walks on water.

And there is part of me that wishes the story ended there with closing credits. But there is another part of me that is glad that it doesn't.

> When [Peter] saw the wind, he was afraid and beginning to sink, cried out, "Lord, save me!"

Let me tell you something about stepping out in faith: You almost always second guess yourself. You make the decision to get out of the boat—you change careers or end a relationship or invest in a stock—and you have second thoughts. You wonder if you made a mistake. *Did God really tell me to get out of the boat?*

And you start sinking spiritually because you stop focusing on Jesus and start focusing on the wind and the waves.

In January of 2003 I cast the multisite vision for our church to our congregation. At our Annual Leadership Retreat, I told our leaders that we were going to step out in faith and launch a second location in a movie theater at a metro stop somewhere in the DC area in the fall of that year. Then I cast the vision to our congregation the next day in my annual "State of the Church" message.

I was full of vision on Saturday and Sunday, but I was second guessing myself the very next day. The Monday blues is a common occurrence with preachers, but I hit bottom. Here is what I wrote in my journal:

Once I cast the vision for the launch, I had this feeling like, "Wow, we really need to do this now." It was that "scary, uneasy" feeling that you get every time you try something you've never done before.

I'll never forget sitting at a Starbucks on the first floor of Ballston Common Mall in Arlington, Virginia, shortly thereafter and reading a book by Andy Stanley titled *The Next Generation Leader*. The timing was divine. Have you ever read something and felt like it was written exclusively for you? I opened the book to a chapter on uncertainty and read what Andy Stanley wrote:

Generally speaking, you are probably never going to be more than 80 percent certain. Waiting for greater certainty may cause you to miss an opportunity.

It's hard to explain, but that released me from the second thoughts I was having. I stopped focusing on the wind and waves and refocused on what God was calling us to do. I knew that no matter how risky or how difficult it was, launching another location was what we were supposed to be doing.

Most of us want absolute certainty before we step out in faith. We love 100-percent money-back guarantees. But the problem with that is this: It takes faith out of the equation. There is no such thing as risk-free faith. And you can't experience success without risking failure.

Sink or Sit

Peter gets a bum rap. Peter is the disciple who denied Christ three times, but he was the only one who got close enough to Jesus to get caught. Peter is the disciple who impulsively cut off Malchus' ear when the lynch mob came to arrest Jesus, but he was the only one who came to Jesus' defense. And he is the disciple who sinks in the Sea of Galilee, but he was also the only disciple who walked on water.

It's so easy to criticize Peter from the comfortable confines of the boat.

I think there are two kinds of people in the world: creators and criticizers. There are people who get out of the boat and walk on water. And there are people who sit in the boat and criticize water walkers.

Here is what I think: Sinking is better than sitting.

I'd rather get wet than have a numb gluteus maximus. When everything is said and done, I think our greatest regrets will be the God-ordained risks we didn't take. We won't regret sinking. We will regret sitting. In the words of German author Johann Wolfgang von Goethe, "Hell begins the day God grants you the vision to see all that you could have done, should have done, and would have done, but did not do."

Anything less than getting out of the boat is spiritual voyeurism. It is so easy to criticize water walkers from the comfortable confines of the boat. But I think the other eleven disciples were haunted by this missed opportunity. Think about it. They could have walked on water. But they chose to stay in the boat. They missed a once-in-a-lifetime opportunity because they weren't willing to take a God-ordained risk.

Inaction Regrets

Remember the regrets of action and regrets of inaction from chapter 1? A regret of action is doing something you wish you hadn't done. A regret of inaction is not doing something that you wish you had done.

I have my fair share of action regrets. I felt really bad about sending my next-door neighbor to the emergency room with a BB lodged in his upper thigh when I was in junior high. I honestly didn't think my aim would be that accurate out of my second-story bedroom window. He had to be fifty yards away, and my Daisy BB gun didn't even have a scope. Unfortunately, I'm a better shot than I realized. I'll never forget the sound of the doorbell ringing about twenty-seven seconds after one of the dumbest decisions of my life. I had action regret. I felt like slapping my forehead with the palm of my hand while repeating, "Stupid, stupid, stupid."

All of us have said things and done things that we regret. We wish we could hit the rewind button and undo what we did. Who hasn't secretly wanted the ability to fly counter-rotational around the earth at supersonic speeds and reverse time like Superman?

All of us have action regrets, but I think our deepest regrets are missed opportunities. Action regrets taste bad, but inaction regrets leave a bitter aftertaste that lasts a lifetime. Inaction regrets haunt us because they leave us asking, "What if?" We wonder how our lives would have been different had we taken the risk or seized the opportunity. What if we had chased the lion instead of running away? Somehow our lives seem incomplete. Failing to take a risk is almost like losing a piece of the jigsaw puzzle of your life. It leaves a gaping hole. When we get to the end of our lives, our greatest regrets will be the missing pieces.

That conviction is backed up by the research of two Cornell social psychologists named Tom Gilovich and Vicki Medvec. Their research found that time is a key factor in what we regret. We usually regret our actions over the short-term. But over the long haul, we tend to regret inactions. Their study found that in an average week, action regrets were slightly greater than inaction regrets—53 percent to 47 percent. But when people look at their lives as a whole, inaction regrets outnumber action regrets 84 percent to 16 percent.[2]

Most of us regret sins of commission in the short-term. But it's the sins of omission, the missed opportunities, that haunt us the rest of our lives. We won't regret the mistakes we made as much as the God-ordained opportunities we missed. In other words, what we'll regret most at the end of our lives are the lions we *didn't* chase.

A few years ago, National Community Church helped build a Teen Challenge Center in Ocho Rios, Jamaica. After completing our mission, our family stayed in Jamaica for a few days to relax and enjoy the island. We were staying near Montego Bay, but I picked up a tourist brochure about cliff jumping in Negril. The second I saw it I knew I needed to do it. But we kept finding excuses. Before I knew it, I was on a plane headed home, and I remember thinking to myself, *I might never get back here.* I still regret not jumping off those cliffs. In fact, one of my dreams is to do a cliff baptism. Talk about baptism by immersion! I still feel like I forfeited a once-in-a-lifetime experience.

In the big scheme of things, this regret isn't life shattering. It's rather benign. But it still haunts me. I still regret not jumping off that cliff.

If you're anything like me, your jigsaw puzzle has some missing pieces. You have some inaction regrets. So what do you do with them? You can wallow in self-pity. You can beat yourself up. You can drown in a pool of regret. Or you can channel those regrets into a more courageous approach to life. You can resolve to chase the lion you ran away from last time. Fight for your second marriage. Take your next pregnancy to full term. Reapply for the program. Try out for *American Idol* the next season.

Henry David Thoreau offered timeless advice when it comes to redeeming regret:

> Make the most of your regrets; never smother your sorrow, but tend and cherish it till it comes to have a separate and integral interest. To regret deeply is to live afresh.

Chicken

It was about one year ago that I was invited to speak at a community meeting on Capitol Hill and give an update on our coffeehouse project. We had just started construction on Ebenezers and a group of community leaders wanted to hear more about our plans. I gave a progress report, cast some vision, and then I fielded questions.

One of the questions put me on the defensive. Someone asked me what the name Ebenezers meant. Instead of coming right out and saying that it was a Hebrew word from I Samuel 7:12 that means "Hitherto the Lord hath helped us," I chickened out. I said, "It basically means, so far so good." But that isn't what it means because that takes God out of the equation.

Now let me put this story in context.

I was in a defensive mindset for a couple reasons. In too many instances, "Christian coffeehouse" is an oxymoron. I've seen lots of Christian coffeehouses that don't do justice to Christianity or coffee. And I was concerned about the negative perceptions people might have if they thought our coffeehouse was going to be one of those.

One other factor that put me on the defensive was one of the people who happened to be in attendance. A few weeks earlier we had hosted our annual Easter egg hunt on Capitol Hill, and one of the guests complained. She said we were talking about Jesus too much. God forbid! We explained that we had totally funded the event, we had permits from the park service, and we are a *church* after all. Plus there are these cornerstones of democracy known as freedom of speech and freedom of religion. But that didn't pacify her antagonism towards us. Long story short, this woman was at the community meeting. And I think it put me in a defensive posture subconsciously. So instead of offending this woman, I offended *the Holy Spirit* by taking God out of the equation of our coffeehouse.

I went home, and I felt so convicted by the Holy Spirit and my wife. Thank God for a godly wife who can speak the truth in love. I apologized to God because I knew that I had chickened out. And I promised that I wouldn't take Him out of the equation any more. I promised that I wouldn't be defensive about my relationship with Him. I promised that I would unapologetically and unashamedly give credit where credit is due.

That experience was a defining moment for me. I could have beaten myself up for chickening out. But I channeled that regret into a new resolve to chase lions whenever they cross my path.

Crash Helmets

There are basically two approaches to life: playing to win and playing not to lose. Can you guess which camp lion chasers fall into? Too many of us are tentatively playing the game of life as if the purpose of life is to arrive safely at death. We need to take our cues from the early believers who competed for the Kingdom.

> "From the days of John the Baptist until now, the kingdom of heaven has been forcefully advancing, and forceful men lay hold of it."

There is nothing remotely passive about following Christ. Some of us approach our relationship with Christ like we're called to play a "prevent defense" when we ought to be in a "two-minute offense." Some of us act like faithfulness is making no turnovers when faithfulness is scoring touchdowns. Faithfulness has nothing to do with maintaining the status quo or holding the fort. It has everything to do with competing for the Kingdom and storming the gates of Hell. With a squirt gun, if necessary!

This past year I coached my son's fourth-grade basketball team. At the beginning of the season, most of the kids didn't know how to play the game. They had zero basketball instincts. In fact, the beginnings of games were pure chaos. Despite repeated attempts to point them in the right direction, most of the kids didn't know which basket to defend and which one to shoot at. Occasionally, our kids would play defense on the offensive side and offense on the defensive side. Sometimes our kids were totally oblivious to the fact that we had the ball, so I yelled at the top of my lungs: "You're on offense! You're on offense!"

Sometimes I wonder if the cloud of witnesses sitting in the celestial bleachers is yelling: "You're on offense! You're on offense!"

Jesus commissioned the church in Matthew 16:18: "I will build my church and the gates of hell will not overcome it."

Gates are defensive devices. Storming those gates requires offensive measures. Think of the church as a battering ram.

In her book *Teaching a Stone to Talk*, Annie Dillard strikes a nerve in her description of the church.

On the whole, I do not find Christians, outside of the catacombs, sufficiently sensible of conditions. Does anyone have the foggiest idea what sort of power we so blithely invoke? Or as I suspect, does no one believe a word of it? The churches are children playing on the floor with their chemistry sets, mixing up a batch of TNT to kill a Sunday morning.

It is madness to wear ladies' straw hats and velvet hats to church; we should all be wearing crash helmets. Ushers should issue life preservers and signal flares; they should lash us to our pews. For the sleeping god may wake someday and take offense, or the waking god may draw us out to where we can never return.[3]

Is anybody else tired of the church playing defense? Why is it that the church is known more for what we're against than what we're for? Why does it seem like the church is always in a defensive posture? Maybe it's time for Christ followers to put on crash helmets and play offense.

God is raising up a generation of lion chasers that don't just run away from evil. God is raising up a generation of lion chasers that have the courage to compete for the kingdom.

I have the joy of pastoring a lot of lion chasers. Most of them do what they do in relative obscurity. You won't see them on *Larry King Live* or *Oprah*. But they are courageously making a difference in their respective callings.

I think of legislative directors and press secretaries working in congressional offices drafting legislation and strategizing campaigns. I think of a former NCC intern who is majoring in film and feels as called to Hollywood as I do to DC. I think of the actors and artists who are making a difference on stage and off stage. I think of the teachers who could be making more money in better school districts, but they feel called to work in the DC public school system. I think of the journalists in our congregation that produce the shows we watch and write the stories we read. I think of a friend that sits on the board of six charities that are leveraging their resources to make a holy difference. And I think of a former intern for a Supreme Court justice who might just land a seat there someday.

Lion chasers don't retreat. They attack. Lion chasers aren't reactors. They are creators. Lion chasers refuse to live their lives in a defensive posture. They are actively looking for ways to make a difference.

In his book *Roaring Lambs*, Bob Briner reflects on missionary conventions he went to as a kid where children were challenged to commit themselves to missions. And that's an awesome thing. Missionaries are heroes. But I agree with Briner when he says that the same spirit needs to prevail in sending our children into culture-shaping professions like entertainment, journalism, education, and politics.

I envision a whole generation who will lay claim to these careers with the same vigor and commitment that sent men like Hudson Taylor to China.

Why not believe that one day the most critically acclaimed director in Hollywood could be an active Christian layman in his church? Why not hope that the Pulitzer Prize for investigative reporting could go to a Christian journalist on staff at a major daily newspaper? Is it really too much of a stretch to think that a major exhibit at the Museum of Modern Art could feature the works of an artist on staff at one of our fine Christian colleges? Am I out of my mind to suggest that your son or daughter could be the principle dancer for the Joffrey Ballet Company, leading a weekly Bible study for other dancers in what was once considered a profession that was morally bankrupt?[4]

We need to stop criticizing culture and start creating it.

Paul didn't boycott the Aeropagus. He didn't stand outside with a picket sign: "Athenian Idolaters Are Going to Hell in a Hand Basket." Paul wasn't playing not to lose. Paul was playing to win, so he went toe-to-toe with some of the greatest philosophical minds in the ancient world. Paul competed for the truth on their turf.

Instead of complaining about the current state of affairs, we need to offer better alternatives. We need to make better movies and better music. We need to write better books. We need to start better schools and better businesses.

As the old aphorism suggests, we need to *stop cursing the darkness* and *start lighting some candles!*

In the words of Michelangelo, we need to *criticize by creating*. And you can't create without taking a calculated risk.

Chapter 6 Review

Points to Remember

- Small changes and small choices become magnified over time and have major consequences.
- Sometimes taking a calculated risk means giving up something good so you can experience something great.
- One courageous choice may be the only thing between you and your dream becoming reality.
- The goal of faith is *not* the elimination of risk.
- A relationship with God is the ultimate win/win relationship because you can *never* give up more than you get back.
- We won't regret the mistakes we made as much as the God-ordained opportunities we missed.
- There is nothing passive about following Christ.

Starting Your Chase

Mark says, "There is no such thing as risk-free faith." What risks are stopping you from tackling an important task or growing in an important area in your life right now?

CHAPTER 7

Grab Opportunity
by the Mane

People are always blaming their circumstances
for what they are. I don't believe in circumstances.
The people who get on in this world are the people
who get up and look for the circumstances they
want, and if they can't find them, they make them.

George Bernard Shaw

It was about a year ago that I had lunch with John, a
Georgetown lawyer who attends National Community
Church. On paper, it looked like John had it made. He had a
well-established law practice making great money. But there
was one nagging problem. Or should I say opportunity? He
didn't want to practice law any more. He wanted to make
movies.

John told me about his dream over lunch, and it sounded
just crazy enough to qualify as a God thing. Crazy career
changes seem to be part and parcel of following Christ. Jesus
himself was practicing carpentry before he went into ministry.

We talked about some of the challenges he would face and
some of the sacrifices he would have to make. But it seemed

like there was a circumstantial convergence happening in his life that made this calling unmistakable. In fact, I still remember the analogy he used. He said it felt like the Rubik's Cube was about to be solved. I wouldn't know how that feels. I've never actually solved one of those things! But I liked the analogy. So we prayed that God would open a door of opportunity. I picked up the tab. And we went back to our daily routines.

A few months later, John was reading the Sunday edition of the *Washington Post*, and a story on human trafficking in Uganda didn't just get his attention, it got in his spirit. Little girls were (and still are) being lured into a life of sexual slavery despite the Ugandan government's attempts to combat the practice with chastity scholarships. My friend could have thrown the paper in the recycling bin and forgotten about it. But he felt like he needed to do something. So he Googled Uganda. That Google search led him down a cyber rabbit trail to a professor who was leading a trip to Uganda to shoot documentary films. Despite the fact that he had no experience and no equipment, my friend applied for the program. And his up-front honesty about his lack of qualifications was his ticket to Uganda. The professor said, "Because you told me the truth, you can come."

I'll never forget John's phone call after getting accepted to the program. It is one of those conversations that is etched into my cerebral cortex. My friend was excited about the opportunity, but there were lots of questions and concerns. To be honest, he wasn't sure if he should go or not. He wasn't sure his vaccinations would take effect in time for the trip. He didn't know if he could get a visa that quickly. And he had second thoughts about leaving his wife and kids behind for three weeks. We weighed the pros and cons. We counted the costs as best we could. But at the end of the conversation, it seemed like this might be a God-ordained opportunity. The serendipitous events seemed to have God's fingerprints all over them. And the story gets even better.

One week before leaving for Uganda, John was invited to a film-industry party. He didn't want to go. He was physically exhausted from preparing for the trip, and he still had a million details to tie up before leaving the country. But his wife felt like he needed to be there. In fact, she prayed that he'd make one significant contact. Call me crazy, but if you're headed to Uganda to shoot a documentary film, I'd say that Uganda's ambassador to the U.S. qualifies as a significant contact. Not only did my friend meet the Ugandan ambassador at the party, but also, as a Christ follower, she felt such an affinity for his film project that she invited him to meet with her at the Ugandan Embassy the next day.

Can you imagine John trying to make an appointment with the Ugandan ambassador out of the blue? What would be the chances of actually getting in to see her? But God is in the business of making sure we cross paths with the right people at the right time. The Holy Spirit can open doors that seem to be dead bolted shut. As my friend's wife said, "Jesus Christ is the ultimate Washington insider."

Long story short, John spent three weeks shooting his documentary film and three months editing and producing it. Then, just a few weeks ago, we had the privilege of hosting the premier showing of his thirty-minute documentary film titled *Sing*.

And the story doesn't end there.

John called me last week and told me that he just got his first movie deal. He'll work as an assistant director and producer on a $20 million feature film. Someday you are going to see his name in the movie credits at the end of a film or maybe you'll even see him accepting an Oscar.

All I can say is this: Crazy dreams still come true. If God can turn bodybuilders into judges or fishermen into apostles or shepherds into kings, then he can most definitely turn lawyers into movie producers.

Now let me make an observation. I've seen it countless times in the lives of others and in my own life. Dreams usually start out as mustard-seed opportunities. In fact, the biggest dreams often start out as the smallest opportunities. The seed is so small you wonder if it can actually grow into anything of significance.

For my friend it was a story in a newspaper. He could have skipped right over that article. He could have ignored the plight of human trafficking. He could have thought to himself, *I wish someone would do something about that.* But a seed was planted in his spirit. And a God-ordained Google search revealed a unique opportunity.

My friend was scared. The opportunity involved lots of sacrifices. And it was downright risky. But lion chasers recognize a God-ordained opportunity when they see one. And they are willing to chase opportunities halfway around the world if that is what God is calling them to do.

Mustard Seeds

Our ultimate destiny is determined by whether or not we seize the God-ordained opportunities presented to us. If we seize those opportunities, the dominos continue to fall and create a chain reaction. But if we miss those opportunities, we short-circuit God's plan for our lives. That doesn't mean we should live in fear that we'll somehow miss the will of God. He'll keep giving us second and third and fourth chances.

Forty years after a felony made Moses a fugitive, God reopened the door of opportunity and gave him a second chance. The grace of God has no expiration date. God will keep opening doors of opportunity as long as we live. But I don't want to delay the process forty years, do you? Life is too short. I want to seize the opportunity the first time it is presented.

Now put yourself in Benaiah's sandals.

This story could have been scripted so differently. Benaiah sees lion. Benaiah runs away. Benaiah breathes a huge sigh of relief.

No harm. No foul.

Running away from the lion may have even been the logical thing to do. Some would have called it prudent. But guess what? Benaiah would have disappeared into the annals of history and been lost amongst the timid souls who shrank back in fear instead of stepping out in faith.

There is certainly a time to be prudent. But there is also a time to be valiant.

I know lots of prudent people. They pay their taxes on time. They drive the speed limit. And they always pack an extra pair of underwear. I respect these people. But that level of respect doesn't begin to compare with the respect I have for valiant people.

Benaiah could have done what was prudent and run away from the lion. I'm sure there was a voice in the back of his head saying "wouldn't be prudent" to chase the lion. But Scripture doesn't describe Benaiah as being prudent. It uses the adjective *valiant*.

Lion chasers aren't the most prudent people on the planet. Lion chasers are opportunists. Lion chasers aren't focused on avoiding problems. Their modus operandi is seizing God-ordained opportunities. And like my friend, the lawyer-turned-moviemaker, they typically start out as mustard-seed opportunities.

Benaiah had to prove himself like everybody else. He started out as a bodyguard for the King of Israel. It was a low-ranking position in the administration that barely paid enough to keep food on the table. He probably had to work a second job. But he evidently proved himself in that capacity because he was appointed an army commander and given leadership over a division of twenty-four thousand men. And Benaiah must have proved himself again, because David's successor, Solomon, appointed Benaiah commander in chief over Israel's entire army.

How did Benaiah fulfill his destiny and realize his dream? How did he climb the military chain of command all the way to the top of the ladder? How did he become the most powerful person in Israel next to the king himself?

He did it by seizing one opportunity at a time.

What we fail to realize is that Benaiah had to put together a résumé, supply references, go through an interview, and get security clearance before getting the bodyguard position.

Nothing has changed in three thousand years. Dreams are still achieved one opportunity at a time.

So here is my advice. Don't just settle for prudence. Strive for valiance. Make the call. Apply for the program. Send the e-mail. Hand in your resignation. Set up the meeting.

The genealogy of success always traces back to mustard seed opportunities. Make the most of them. For what it's worth, I think many of us fail to seize the small opportunities because we're looking for the big opportunities. But Scripture says, "Do not despise these small beginnings."

Benaiah started out as a bodyguard. Joshua was a personal assistant. Elisha was an intern. And Nehemiah was a cupbearer.

You've got to prove yourself when the little opportunities present themselves. And when you do, God will bring bigger and better opportunities your way.

Opportunity Stewardship

You've probably never heard of him before. His name is only mentioned in one verse in one chapter in one book of the Bible. But that one verse speaks volumes. He is a biblical footnote, but like Benaiah, he does something pretty remarkable. He single-handedly delivers the Israelites from the Philistines.

> After Ehud came Shamgar, son of Anath, who struck down
> six hundred Philistines with an oxgoad. He too saved Israel.

As far as we know, Shamgar had no armor, no military training, and no weapons. There is nothing that qualified him to do what he did. Shamgar was a plowman. And all he had was an oxgoad, a long stick used to prod oxen while plowing.

When you are choosing weapons to wage war, an oxgoad doesn't even make the list. Just imagine what Shamgar could have done with a real weapon like a sword or a spear. But Shamgar didn't have a sword or a spear. All he had was an oxgoad. He just did the best he could with what he had.

Shamgar and Benaiah are kindred spirits. Both of them displayed epic courage. Both of them defied the odds. Both of them changed the course of history. And both of them could have found a logical excuse for noninvolvement.

Shamgar was outnumbered six hundred to one. And all he had was an oxgoad.

The Egyptian had a spear the size of a weaver's rod. And all Benaiah had was a club.

But lion chasers don't look for excuses. They don't focus on disadvantages. They find a way of making circumstances work in their favor. If need be, they put the Egyptian into a half nelson and wrench the spear out of his hand.

Isn't it ironic that some people who have so much do *so little* and others who have so little do *so much*? Lion chasers don't let what they *can't* do keep them from doing what they *can*.

I have a simple definition of success. Success is doing the best you can with what you have where you are. In a sense, success is relative. Success is as unique as your fingerprint. It looks different for different people depending on your circumstances and gifts. But there is one common denominator that I see in all successful people. They can spot an opportunity a mile away. And they seize the opportunity with both hands. They grab life by the mane. And that is what opportunity stewardship is all about.

Think of every opportunity as a gift from God. What you do with that opportunity is your gift *to* God.

Make the most of every opportunity.

This Scripture doesn't specify how many or how few opportunities. It doesn't quantify how small or how large the opportunity. We simply need to make the most of *every* opportunity.

The word translated *opportunity* is the Greek word *kairos*. It refers to "a serendipitous window of opportunity." Seeing and seizing opportunities is an overlooked and underappreciated dimension of spiritual maturity. Every day is filled with countless God-ordained opportunities. Not a day goes by that we don't have an opportunity to love, an opportunity to serve, an opportunity to give, or an opportunity to learn.

But there is a catch. The old aphorism is wrong. Opportunity doesn't knock. Opportunity roars!

Most of us want our opportunities nicely packaged and presented to us as a gift we simply have to unwrap. We want our lions stuffed or caged or cooked medium well and served on a silver platter. But opportunities typically present themselves at the most inopportune time in the most inopportune place.

The two Moabites didn't schedule an appointment with Benaiah's assistant. The Egyptian didn't knock *on* the door. He knocked *down* the door. And the lion didn't roll over and play dead.

Here is the great irony about opportunities. They usually come disguised as insurmountable problems. They look like five-hundred-pound lions that want to eat you for lunch. Or they look like six hundred Philistines charging at you.

To the average person, the circumstances presented to Benaiah were problems to run away from, not opportunities to be seized. But

Benaiah didn't see a five-hundred-pound problem. He saw a lion skin hanging in his tent.

Lion chasers are the kind of people who rise to the occasion. Lion chasers are the kind of people who refuse to be intimidated by Moabites or Philistines. Lion chasers play to win. They fight for what they believe in. They don't live life sitting back on their heels. They live life on the tip of their toes waiting to see what God is going to do next.

The Reticular Activating System

Part of me wonders if Benaiah learned how to pray from David. It would make sense, wouldn't it? As his bodyguard, Benaiah never left David's side. When David went into his prayer closet, Benaiah was the one guarding the door. He couldn't help but overhear what David was praying about. For that matter, David strikes me as the kind of guy who would pray with his staff. Prayer was part of the warp and woof of David's daily routine. And I think it rubbed off on Benaiah. I think Benaiah learned how to live in prayer mode from the prayer warrior himself, King David.

Psalm 5:3 reveals the way David started every day: "In the morning, O LORD, you hear my voice; in the morning I lay my requests before you and wait in expectation."

One of our greatest spiritual shortcomings is *low expectations*. We don't expect much from God because we aren't asking for much.

When my prayer life is hitting on all eight cylinders, I can believe God for everything. But when I'm in a prayer slump, I have a hard time believing God for anything. Low expectations are the byproduct of prayerlessness, but prayer has a way of God-sizing our expectations. David can't wait to see what God is going to do next because he is living in prayer mode. The more you pray, the higher your expectations.

Not only does prayer sanctify expectations. It creates cognitive categories.

Let me try to explain how it works neurologically.

At the base of our brain stem there is a cluster of nerve cells called the reticular activating system (RAS). We are constantly bombarded by countless stimuli—sights and sounds and smells. If we had to process or pay attention to all the stimuli, it would drive us crazy. The RAS determines what gets noticed and what goes unnoticed. Think of it as your mental radar system.

An interesting thing happened when I started writing *In a Pit with a Lion on a Snowy Day*. I was writing about and thinking about lions so much that I started noticing lions every place I looked. I noticed lion logos. I noticed how many T-shirts have lion designs. And I noticed lion statues in front of countless DC buildings. I'm sure they were there all along, but I hadn't noticed them. Why? Because I wasn't looking for them. I didn't have a cognitive category for lions. So what happened? *In a Pit with a Lion on a Snowy Day* created a category in my reticular activating system. I now notice lions whenever and wherever I see them.

You've experienced the same phenomenon with everything you own. When you purchase a cell phone or clothing or a car, it creates a category in your reticular activating system. You notice if someone's cell phone has the same ring tone, don't you? Because you go to answer yours. You notice if someone is wearing your outfit at the same event. (Can you say awkward?) And the second you drive your new car out of the lot it seems like everyone is driving the same model.

That is the function of the RAS. You didn't have a category for your clothing or ring tone or car before you bought them. But once you made the purchase or downloaded the ring tone or drove out of the dealership, you had a new cognitive category.

So what does that have to do with prayer?

When we pray for someone or something, it creates a category in our reticular activating system. Prayer is important for the same reason goals are important. We need to create categories so we will notice anything and everything that helps us achieve those goals or answer those prayers. As I remind our congregation all the time: It all comes back to the reticular activating system. If you want to see and seize God-ordained opportunities, you've got to live in prayer mode.

In a sense, Benaiah's heroic acts of courage were unplanned. But don't think that Benaiah was unprepared. He couldn't predict when, how, or where the lion encounter would happen, but he had been preparing for it since he was a boy. Can't you see Benaiah wrestling with his poor pet cat that doubled as an imaginary lion? He practiced his swordsmanship in front of a mirror until it became second nature. And he staged faux battles with his brothers. So when the lion crossed his path he didn't see it as *bad luck*. He saw it for what it was: *a divine appointment*. He literally seized the opportunity. The lion didn't take Benaiah by surprise. He had been waiting for it his entire life.

Carpe feline.

Prayer Mode

Devote yourselves to prayer, being watchful and thankful.

If you want to make the most of every opportunity you've got to "devote yourselves to prayer, being watchful."

The word *watchful* is a throwback to the Old Testament watchmen whose job it was to sit on the city wall, scan the horizon, and keep watch. They were the first ones to see an attacking army or traveling traders. People who live in prayer mode are watchmen. They see further than others see. They see things before others see them. And they see things other people don't see.

People who live in prayer mode see opportunities that other

people don't even notice. People who don't live in prayer mode are *opportunity blind*.

There are only two ways to live your life: survival mode or prayer mode.

Survival mode is simply reacting to the circumstances around you. It is a pinball existence. And to be perfectly honest, it's predictable, monotonous, and boring.

Prayer mode is the exact opposite. Your spiritual antenna is up and your radar is on. Your reticular activating system is on red alert. Prayer puts you in a proactive posture. In fact, the Aramaic word for prayer, *slotha*, means "to set a trap." Prayer helps us catch the opportunities God throws our way.

If Benaiah had been in survival mode, he would have reacted to the situation by running away from the lion. But living in prayer mode made him proactive. He knew that God was ordering his footsteps even when they crossed paths with paw prints. He knew that the lion was lunch.

Living in prayer mode is the difference between seeing *coincidences* and *providences*. Prayer has a way of helping us recognize that what we might dismiss as human accidents are really divine appointments. All I know from personal experience is this: When I pray, providences happen. When I don't pray, they don't happen.

Now let me take some of the pressure off. You don't have to manufacture opportunities. In fact, you can't manufacture them. That's part of God's portfolio. He is preparing good works in advance. And that ought to give us a tremendous sense of destiny. You will have plenty of God-ordained opportunities. Your job is to see and seize those opportunities by tuning in to the still, small voice of the Holy Spirit. And you'll be amazed at the way those spirit whispers get you where God wants you to go.

When National Community Church was getting off the ground, our church office was a spare bedroom in our house. Then our

daughter, Summer, was born, and that room doubled as office by day
and bedroom by night. We would set up and tear down her portable
crib every day, but that got real old real fast, so we started aggressively
looking for office space for the church. Over the course of the next
four months we found two places that seemed to be perfect, and we
put contracts on both of them—but both contracts fell through. It
honestly felt like God had pulled the carpet out from under our feet
twice.

Then I was walking home from Union Station one day, and I
passed in front of a row house at 205 F Street, NE. There was no
"For Sale" sign or "For Rent" sign, but I felt prompted to call the
owner. Somehow the Holy Spirit surfaced his name out of the recesses
of my subconscious. That is the only way I can describe it. I had met
the owner a year before, but I'm not great with names. To be honest,
I wasn't one-hundred-percent sure the name that surfaced was really
the owner's name, but I looked it up in the phone book and dialed
the number.

I introduced myself, and before I could tell him why I was calling,
he interrupted me and said, "I was just thinking about you. In fact, I
was going to give you a call. I'm thinking about putting 205 F Street
on the market, and I was wondering if you'd be interested."

God's timing is impeccable!

Not only did we purchase 205 F Street, but it gave us a foothold
on the adjacent property at 201 F Street. I can't tell you how many
times we laid hands on those brick walls at 205 F Street and asked
God to give us the adjoining property. That adjoining property is now
Ebenezers Coffeehouse. And if things go according to plan, it will be
the first of many. But no matter how many coffeehouses we open, it
will all trace back to a prompting of the Holy Spirit while I was in
prayer mode.

As I look back on my life, the greatest breakthroughs have
happened while I've been in prayer mode. Prayer is an opportunity

incubator. When I'm not in prayer mode, I have *good* ideas. But when I'm in prayer mode I have *God* ideas. And I'd rather have one God idea than a thousand good ideas.

Swallow the Whale

In my estimation, Jeremiah 46:17 is one of the saddest verses in Scripture: "Pharaoh king of Egypt is only a loud noise; he has missed his opportunity."

The pharaoh ruled over one of the most advanced ancient civilizations on earth. Think of his influence. Think of his wealth. The resources of an entire kingdom were at his disposal. But he missed his moment. The opportunity came and went without Pharaoh seeing it or seizing it. What a waste.

The English word *opportunity* comes from the Latin phrase *ob portu*. In the days before modern harbors, ships had to wait till flood tide to make it into port. The Latin phrase ob portu referred to "that moment in time when the tide would turn." The captain and crew would wait for that window of opportunity to open, and they knew that if they missed it, they would have to wait for another tide to come in.

Shakespeare borrowed the concept in one of his famous verses from *Julius Ceasar*:

There is a tide in the affairs of men
Which, taken at the flood, leads on to fortune.
Omitted, all the voyage of their life
Is bound in shallows and in miseries.
On such a full sea we are now afloat;
And we must take the current when it serves,
Or lose our ventures.

In August of 1987, Howard Schultz was faced with the biggest decision of his life. He was presented with an opportunity to purchase a small chain of coffee shops called Starbucks. The price tag was $4 million. To Schultz, it seemed like an overwhelming undertaking. He said it felt like a case of "the salmon swallowing the whale."[1]

Schultz reflects on his decision in his autobiography, *Pour Your Heart into It*:

> *This is my moment*, I thought. *If I don't seize the opportunity, if I don't step out of my comfort zone and risk it all, if I let too much time tick on, my moment will pass.* I knew that if I didn't take advantage of this opportunity, I would replay it in my mind for my whole life, wondering: *What if?*[2]

Schultz decided to give up seventy-five thousand dollars in income so he could pursue his coffee passion. And as they say, the rest is history.

Starbucks stock went public on June 26, 1992. It was the second most actively traded stock on the NASDAQ, and by the closing bell, its market capitalization stood at $273 million. Not bad for a $4 million investment.[3]

Seizing an opportunity usually feels like swallowing a whale or chasing a lion. But at the end of our lives, we won't regret the mistakes we made nearly as much as the opportunities we missed. It will be the "what if" questions that haunt us.

What if Howard Schultz hadn't swallowed the whale?

It's hard to even imagine life without a Starbucks on every street corner in every city in the galaxy, isn't it? Our lives would be so inconvenienced if there wasn't a Starbucks at every gate in every airport in the civilized world.

In the business world, missed opportunities are called "opportunity costs." If Howard Schultz had decided not to purchase Starbucks, it would not have cost him one red cent in actual costs. In fact, he would have saved $4 million dollars. But the opportunity costs would have been staggering.

In the long run, opportunity costs are always more damaging than actual costs.

Far too many people think of righteousness in terms of actual costs instead of opportunity costs. We mistakenly think of righteousness as *doing nothing wrong* when, in fact, righteousness is *doing something right*. Righteousness isn't just running away from sin. Righteousness is chasing lions.

Throw Caution to the Wind

I'm a recovering perfectionist. I have a hard time tying off the umbilical cord on anything, but I've found that Ecclesiastes 11:1 is a great prescription for perfectionism. And it is one key to seizing opportunities. "Cast your bread upon the waters, for after many days you will find it again."

There is a time to be cautious and a time to throw caution to the wind. There is a time to test the waters and a time to cast your bread upon the water. There is a time to be prudent and a time to be valiant. And it takes tremendous discernment to know the difference. But I know this for sure: If you wait for perfect conditions before you seize an opportunity, you'll be waiting till the day you die.

Whoever watches the wind will not plant; whoever looks at the clouds will not reap.

More often than not, the only thing between you and your dream is a rational excuse. My friend could have come up with a hundred reasons not to go to Uganda. But lion chasers are not looking for excuses.

Shamgar could have justified his noninvolvement. *I don't have the right weapon. I could get hurt. I'm a plowman, not a soldier. I don't have the right training. I'm not in charge. I'm outnumbered six hundred to one.*

But Shamgar didn't let what he *couldn't do* keep him from doing what he *could*.

What excuses are you making?

I'm too busy.

I'm not qualified.

I'm too qualified.

I've got too many problems.

I don't have enough money.

I'm not ready yet.

Newsflash: You'll never be ready.

I wasn't ready to pastor a church. I wasn't ready to get married. We weren't ready to have kids. We weren't ready to launch our second location. And we weren't ready to open a coffeehouse.

You're never going to be ready. But you're in good company. Jesus wasn't even ready! Right before his first miracle there is a hint of hesitation: "My time has not yet come." But Jesus had a mom who loved him enough to push him out of the nest.

Maybe it's time to dust off that dream God has given you. Maybe it's time to throw your hat in the ring. What are you waiting for?

In his book, *Jump In!*, Mark Burnett writes about his journey to TV-producer stardom. Burnett is the creator of *Survivor* and *The Apprentice*. He outlines his philosophy of business in the book, and it makes a good life philosophy:

Nothing will ever be...perfect, and nothing can be totally planned. The best you can hope for is to be about half certain of your plan and know that you and the team you've assembled are willing to work hard enough to overcome the inevitable problems as they arrive. And arrive they will. The only thing you can be certain of in business is that the problems you have not thought of will eventually crop up—and always at the worst times.[4]

"The best you can hope for is to be about half certain." That is a pretty good paraphrase of Ecclesiastes 11. So don't watch the wind. Don't look at the clouds. You've got to cast your bread on the waters. After all, the willingness to fail is a prerequisite of success.

Baptism by Immersion

As far as we know, Benaiah didn't take Lion Chasing Skills 101 or Advanced Hand-to-Hand Combat: How to Wrench a Spear Out of the Hand of a Seven-and-a-Half-Foot-Tall Egyptian. And even if he had, I don't think an academic transcript would have landed him the job as David's bodyguard.

There is a difference between a transcript and a résumé. A transcript reveals what you *know*. It's who you are on paper. A résumé reveals what you have *done*. Some of us act as if our transcript is all that matters. But knowledge is not the end goal. What really matters is what we do with what we know. I honestly don't care if you've taken Lion Chasing Skills 101. Have you ever chased a lion into a pit on a snowy day and killed it? I have nothing against a classroom education. I wouldn't trade my undergraduate or graduate education for anything. But there are some lessons that can only be learned outside the classroom environment in the school of hard knocks.

When I felt called to full-time ministry as a nineteen-year-old, I immediately started preaching. I couldn't get any preaching gigs in churches, so I started preaching in homeless shelters and nursing homes.

I'll never forget one of my nursing-home sermons. In the middle of my message, an elderly woman suffering from senility stood up and started taking off her clothes. It's really hard to keep people's attention when a stripper starts stripping in the middle of a service, even if that stripper is eighty-seven years old. Then she started screaming at the top of her lungs: "Get him out of here! Get him out of here!" Not much fazes you after that.

When I went to Bible college, I decided not to just attend a big church and learn by watching. I attended a tiny church that averaged about twelve people in attendance. I wanted to learn by doing. Some of those early messages were pretty pathetic, but that is how I cut my teeth.

When I started pastoring National Community Church, I had zero pastoral experience. I'd only done one summer internship, and all I did was organize the men's softball league. But I wanted to learn how to pastor by pastoring. I made plenty of mistakes, but mistakes are good for you if you learn from them.

I believe in baptism by immersion. The best way to discover what you love to do and what you're good at is to try lots of different things.

Sow your seed in the morning, and at evening let not your
hands be idle, for you do not know which will succeed,
whether this or that, or whether both will do equally well.

For what it's worth, the average college graduate will change jobs ten times. They will also change career paths three to five times. You don't have to get it right the first time. But you do have to sow your seed. You need to start somewhere.

For Benaiah, the dream of becoming Israel's commander in chief started with a lion chase. For Shamgar, it started with an oxgoad. For my friend the moviemaker, it started with a Google search.

I don't know what dream God is calling you to pursue, but I do know this: A dream becomes reality one opportunity at a time. And if you *work like it depends on you* and *pray like it depends on God*, there is no telling what God can do in you and through you.

Chapter 7 Review

Points to Remember

- Our destiny is determined by whether or not we seize the God-ordained opportunities presented to us.
- You've got to prove yourself when the little opportunities present themselves. And when you do, God will bring bigger and better opportunities your way.
- Lion chasers don't let what they *can't* do keep them from doing what they *can*.
- If you want to see and seize God-ordained opportunities, you've got to live in prayer mode.
- If you wait for perfect conditions to seize an opportunity, you'll be waiting till the day you die.
- You don't have to get it right the first time, but you do have to start somewhere. A dream becomes reality one opportunity at a time.

Starting Your Chase

Mark says that a "willingness to fail is a prerequisite to success." Is your fear of failing keeping you from seizing opportunities? What practical steps could you take to become less afraid of failing?

The Importance of Looking Foolish

We try to be too reasonable about what we believe.
What I believe is not reasonable at all. In fact, it's
hilariously impossible. Possible things aren't worth
much. These crazy impossible things keep us going.

MADELEINE L'ENGLE

One of my most embarrassing moments happened in the sixth grade at Madison Junior High School in Naperville, Illinois. I was somewhat fashion-challenged as a kid. But this was a major wardrobe malfunction. I committed the unpardonable clothing faux pas. I wore a neon pink Ocean Pacific shirt to school and paid the price!

I was pretty popular in junior high. My junior-high-school years are filled with great memories and great friends. But I felt lonely and forsaken on the infamous day I wore pinky to school. My friends deserted me. My enemies persecuted me. I didn't get teased very often, but I got my yearlong quota in one day.

I'm not exactly sure what happened to that shirt, but I know that I never wore it again. Why? Because the modus operandi once you hit junior high is *fitting in*. You want to be like everybody else. Call it peer pressure. Call it herd mentality. Call it groupthink. Call it what you want. There is an innate desire within each of us to be accepted at all costs. So we learn at a very early age to become conformists.

We try to *look* like everybody else. We try to *talk* like everybody else. We try to *dress* like everybody else. And the end result? We become like everybody else. We hide our idiosyncrasies and insecurities behind the mask of who we think we're supposed to be. We stop being ourselves and start being who we think everyone wants us to be.

But something invaluable and irreplaceable is lost when we cave in to conformity. We lose our personality. We lose our originality. And at some point we lose our soul. Instead of becoming the one-of-a-kind original we were destined to be, we settle for a carbon copy of someone else.

And when we do, we settle for something less than God intended for us. If you're going to defy the odds, face your fears, reframe your problems, take a risk, and seize a God-ordained opportunity, you have to be willing to look foolish in the world's eyes. Because, no matter how it might look, doing God's will is never foolish.

THE FEAR OF FOOLISHNESS

I believe that somewhere deep down inside all of us there is a primal longing to do something crazy for God. We want to chase a lion like Benaiah. But our fear of looking foolish keeps us hog-tied and locked in the basement.

Poll after poll has found that most people's number one fear is speaking in public. Death ranks number two. That means some people would rather die than speak in public. Why? It is the fear of looking foolish.

It is the fear of foolishness that keeps us from raising our hand in fourth grade. *The other kids will laugh if I get the answer wrong.* It is the fear of foolishness that keeps us from asking someone out on a date. *I don't think I can handle the rejection if they say no.* It is the fear of foolishness that keeps us from changing majors or changing jobs. *People will think I don't know what I want to do.* It is the fear of foolishness that keeps us from praying for a miracle. *What if God doesn't answer my prayer the way I want Him to?*

But here's the deal: If you aren't willing to look foolish, you're foolish. In fact, faith *is* the willingness to look foolish.

Noah looked foolish building an ark in the desert. Sarah looked foolish buying maternity clothes at ninety. The Israelites looked foolish marching around Jericho blowing trumpets. David looked foolish attacking Goliath with a slingshot. Benaiah looked foolish chasing a lion. The wise men looked foolish following yonder star. Peter looked foolish stepping out of the boat in the middle of the lake. And Jesus looked foolish hanging half-naked on the cross.

But that's the essence of faith. And the results speak for themselves.

Noah was saved from the flood. Sarah gave birth to Isaac. The walls of Jericho came tumbling down. David defeated Goliath. Benaiah killed the lion. The wise men found the Messiah. Peter walked on water. And Jesus rose from the dead.

Can I tell you why some people have never killed a giant or walked on water or seen the walls come tumbling down? It's because they weren't willing to look foolish.

I have a catch phrase: "Call me crazy." It's actually become more than a catch phrase. It's become a life motto.

I'm not sure what went through Benaiah's mind right before

chasing the lion. But it wouldn't surprise me if it was "Call me crazy" or "Here goes nothing." Is there anything more foolhardy than chasing a lion? But Benaiah knew this was his moment of truth. Chasing lions went against everything his mother had ever taught him. It is one of the most counterintuitive moves in all of Scripture. It certainly ranks as one of the craziest acts of courage. But maybe that is why God was able to turn this bodyguard into a commander in chief of Israel's army. His "craziness quotient" was off the charts.

The greatest breakthroughs, miracles, and turning points in Scripture can be traced back to someone who was willing to look foolish.

But I Corinthians 1:27 (NLT) reveals God's modus operandi: "God deliberately chose things the world considers foolish in order to shame those who think they are wise."

Nothing has changed.

Divergent Spirituality

I recently read a fascinating study on divergent thinking. Divergent thinking is intellectual originality. It is creative and counterintuitive thought. It is thinking outside the box.

The study found that 98 percent of children between the ages of three and five score in the genius category for divergent thinking. Between the ages of eight and ten, that number drops to 32 percent. By the time the kids become teenagers, it drops down to 10 percent. And only 2 percent of those over twenty-five scored in the genius category for divergent thinking.

According to John Putzier, who cites the study in his book *Get Weird*,[1] the solution to this intellectual conformity and creative atrophy is "tapping your natural weirdness." And I think he's on to something.

Tapping into our natural weirdness isn't just one key to divergent thinking. It is one key to *divergent spirituality.* Have you read the Bible lately? Lots of wild and wacky stuff! At face value, God says and does lots of things that seem awfully weird. He tells Ezekiel to cook his meals over dung for three hundred and ninety days. What's that about? God uses a dumb donkey to speak to Balaam. That's different. God tells Hosea to marry a prostitute. Huh? And what about speaking in tongues on the Day of Pentecost? That's downright strange.

But all of those subplots reveal something important: God loves variety. He speaks and acts in divergent ways.

Can I come right out and say it? Normality is overrated.

Think of it this way. We are called to conform to Christ. And Christ was a nonconformist. So conforming to Christ results in nonconformity.

Too many people in too many churches look too much alike. If anyplace ought to celebrate diversity it ought to be the church. There never has been and never will be anyone like you. And that isn't a testament to you. It's a testament to the God who created you. Diversity is a celebration of originality.

We have a core value at National Community Church: Maturity doesn't equal conformity. In too many churches, holiness is equated with cultural conformity. A dress code or verbal code becomes the measuring stick of righteousness. And as long as you don't say the wrong things or go to the wrong places you're alright. But that's not maturity. That's superficiality. That is skin-deep spirituality. And what you end up with is a herd of cloned Christians that look alike, talk alike, think alike, and dress alike. Not only is that boring, it's not biblical. Scripture describes the church as a body. And each person is a different body part. So we ought to be as different as our big toes, nose hairs, and knee caps.

One dimension of spiritual growth is simply coming to terms with *who we are* and *who we're not.* And at the end of the day, I'd rather be disliked for who I am than liked for who I'm not.

Play the Fool

For more than thirty years, Gordon MacKenzie worked at Hallmark, eventually convincing the company to create a special title for him: "creative paradox." Along with challenging corporate normalcy at Hallmark, MacKenzie did a lot of creativity workshops for elementary schools. And those workshops led to a fascinating observation that he shares in his book, *Orbiting the Giant Hairball.*

MacKenzie would ask the kids upfront: "How many artists are there in the room?" And he said the pattern of responses never varied.

In the first grade, the entire class waved their arms like maniacs. Every child was an artist. In the second grade, about half the kids raised their hands. In the third grade, he'd get about ten out of thirty kids. And by the time he got to sixth grade, only one or two kids would tentatively and self-consciously raise their hands.

All the schools he went to seemed to be involved in "the suppression of creative genius."[2] They weren't doing it on purpose, but society's goal is to make us less foolish. As MacKenzie says, "From the cradle to grave, the pressure is on: Be Normal."[3]

MacKenzie came to this conclusion:

> My guess is that there was a time—perhaps when you were very young—when you had at least a fleeting notion of your own genius and were just waiting for some authority figure to come along and validate it for you.
>
> But none ever came.[4]

Enter Jesus. Our inner fool may be shackled and caged by a world made to suppress it. But Jesus came to free the fool.

I don't think we can understand the full implications of his mission to "proclaim that captives will be released." It means more than freedom from sin. He came to get us out of the psychological straightjacket we've gotten ourselves into. It's about more than the elimination of sin. It's about the redemption of our God-given potential. It's not about not doing anything wrong. It's about making a unique contribution for as many spins on the planet as we get.

But we've got to let the fool out.

The *Los Angeles Times* recently did a story that referenced National Community Church, and the staff writer chose an interesting adjective to describe me. I'm not sure it would have been my first choice. She referred to me as *zany*. In all fairness, she had visited my blog and seen a video of me river dancing in the reflecting pool in front of the Lincoln Memorial. So *zany* was probably a mild choice of adjectives.

I was driving my kids to school the day after the article was printed, and I wanted them to weigh in. I said, "Do you think your daddy is zany?" The response was quick and decisive. A little too quick and a little too decisive!

Summer said, "Uh-huh!" with a big smile.

And Parker added an elongated, "Ohhhh yahhhh!"

I actually looked up the word *zany* in the dictionary, and I had mixed feelings about what I found:

: *fantastically or absurdly ludicrous*

That doesn't exactly sound like a compliment. But maybe it should be. I honestly wonder if we've totally missed what it means to follow in the footsteps of Christ. I'm afraid our version of Christlikeness is way too civilized and sanitized. I wonder if we've turned a blind eye to the zaniness in the Gospels.

Jesus touched lepers, healed on the Sabbath, defended adulterers, befriended prostitutes, washed the feet of his disciples, threw temple tantrums, talked with Samaritans, partied with tax collectors, and regularly offended the Pharirazzi.

Are we really following in His footsteps?

I'm just not convinced that following Christ makes us less zany.

NEOTENY

How do we tap into that zaniness, that natural weirdness we're all born with? We have to return to the time when 98 percent of us were geniuses and we all raised our hands and said we were artists. We've got to take Jesus' advice and "become like little children."

No matter how old David got, there was always a little shepherd boy inside. And even when Benaiah was commander in chief of Israel's army, deep down inside he was still a teenage lion chaser. Lion chasers never grow up.

One of my favorite words is *neoteny*. It derives from the Greek word *neos*, which means "new, fresh, or youthful." Neoteny is "the retention of youthful qualities by adults."

Warren Bennis and Robert Thomas identify neoteny as an indispensable quality of leadership in their book, *Geeks and Geezers*.

Neoteny is more than retaining a youthful appearance, although that is often part of it. Neoteny is the retention of those wonderful qualities that we associate with youth: curiosity, playfulness, eagerness, fearlessness, warmth, energy. Unlike those defeated by time and age, our geezers have remained much like our geeks—open, willing to take risks, hungry for knowledge and experience, courageous, eager to see what the new day brings.[5]

Now here is what you need to understand. Neoteny isn't just a nice concept about people who age well or lead well. Neoteny is at the very heart of what the kingdom of God is all about.

I tell you the truth, unless you change and become like little children you will never enter the kingdom of heaven.

Sir John Kirk, the nineteenth-century British naturalist, once said that if he had his way, there would always be a little child positioned in the heart of London—perhaps in the precincts of Westminster Abbey or St. Paul's Cathedral. And he said that no one would be allowed to contest a seat in Parliament or become a candidate for public office until he had spent a day with that child and passed an examination in the child's novel methods of thought, feeling, and expression.

When I first read that I thought to myself, *What a fascinating idea.* And then I realized that is precisely what Jesus did. He proverbially positioned a child in the heart of the kingdom of heaven. The kingdom of God is child-centric. The way we grow up spiritually is by becoming more and more like a little child.

The word *change* means "to reverse." Jesus came to reverse the curse. And he accomplished that with his crucifixion and resurrection. Jesus paid the penalty for our sin, but that is just the beginning. Jesus came to reverse the psychological and spiritual effects of aging. I love the way one NCCer put it right before her baptism a few years ago: "Now I'm the person I was as a child—always smiling and laughing."

Conversion kick-starts two sanctification processes: Christlikeness and childlikeness. Spiritual maturity is becoming more like Christ and more like a little child.

Recently, Kim, one of our small-group leaders, sent me an e-mail that captures the essence of what it means to be a like a little child.

As parents we set behavioral boundaries for kids, but their potential and imaginations are unlimited. God creates us that way. On any given day, my daughter is planning to grow up to be a princess or a puppy. She is limited by neither genealogy nor genetics. My son will tell you he is going to be a rock star, knight, garbage man, paper boy, astronaut, Jungle Cruise guy, or Aladdin depending on what mood he's in. It doesn't occur to either of them that they can or can't do something!

We internalize limits. We grow up and grow old. What is worse, we become small people with a small God. I think part of Neos is regaining the limitlessness of youth. Regaining the idea that we have been created by a limitless God to have limitless dreams and imaginations.

What limits are you listening to? "I'm too old." "I have a family to think about." "I have too much invested in where I am." "It's too crazy." "It's never been done." "What if I fail?" "It's too expensive." The list goes on forever. Remember this: we serve an unlimited God with unlimited resources. A God who looked at a few loaves and fishes and saw a banquet for five thousand people.

Kids live in a world of limitless possibilities. They dream of growing up to become lion chasers. But we allow the enemy to steal, kill, and destroy those childlike dreams. The key to recapturing those dreams is becoming like little children.

God-Conscious

Whoever humbles himself like this child is the greatest in the kingdom of heaven.

The humility of children is disarming, isn't it? There is no pride or prejudice. There are no inhibitions or hidden agendas. Undiluted humility.

The word *humble* comes from the Greek word *tapeinoo*, which in its strongest form, means "to humiliate." No one is better at that than kids. Why? Because they don't care what people think. They aren't self-conscious yet.

I remember having friends over to our home a few years ago, and my son, Parker, came running through the house yelling, "Captain Underpants!" at the top of his voice. And sure enough, all he had on was underpants. Adults don't do that. Why? Because we're self-conscious! But there is an Eden-like innocence that children possess that all of us crave.

Let me hit the rewind button and take you all the way back to life in the Garden of Eden before the fall of man. It was a nudist colony. Adam and Eve wore their birthday suits all day, every day. And there was no shame. But something happened the split second Adam and Eve stepped outside God's guidelines and ate of the tree of the knowledge of good and evil: "At that moment, their eyes were opened, and they suddenly felt shame at their nakedness."

Before the fall, there were no inhibitions in Eden. But the moment Adam and Eve sinned, they became self-conscious. In other words, self-consciousness isn't just a curse. It is part of The Curse.

Now fast-forward all the way to the last chapter of the book of Revelation. Not only will we receive glorified bodies on the flipside of the space-time continuum, but we'll also receive glorified senses. I think we'll see colors we cannot currently perceive. Our range of hearing will include ultrasonic and infrasonic sound. I think we'll experience new tastes and new fragrances. It will be the most sensual experience we've ever had. And I think a glorified consciousness will be part of the package deal. I don't think there will be any inhibitions in heaven. We'll be far too enraptured with God to waste a single moment thinking about ourselves.

Now think of spiritual maturity as a continuum. On one side is *God-consciousness* and on the other side is *self-consciousness*. To become like Christ is to become less self-conscious and more God-conscious. The end result is the crucifixion of ungodly inhibitions that keep us from chasing lions.

> Don't be drunk with wine.... Instead, let the Holy Spirit fill
> you and control you.

Wine is the wrong way to lose inhibition. The right way is being filled with the Holy Spirit. I like the way priest and author Ron Rolheiser says it:

> Isn't it the task of the Holy Spirit to introduce some madness
> and intoxication into the world? Why this propensity for
> balance and safety? Don't we all long for one moment of raw
> risk, one moment of divine madness?[6]

As I look back on my life, it is the moments of "raw risk" when I came alive.

Maybe it's time to take some childlike chances.

If You're Not Willing to Look Foolish, You're Foolish

As David climbed the political ladder and gained power and prestige, he never lost his ability to look foolish. Even as king, he wasn't afraid to humiliate himself before God. And I think that is why God used David in such epic ways.

In 2 Samuel 6, David has just been crowned King of Israel. He has defeated the Philistines and recaptured Zion. And David is bringing the Ark of the Covenant back to Jerusalem. Think of it as an inaugural parade full of pomp and circumstance.

> But as the Ark of the LORD entered the City of David, Michal, the daughter of Saul, looked down from her window. When she saw King David leaping and dancing before the LORD, she was filled with contempt for him.

Let me make an observation.

When you get excited about God, don't expect everybody to get excited about your excitement. Here's why. When the Holy Spirit turns up the heat underneath you it disrupts the status quo. Some people will be inspired by what God is doing in your life. Others will be convicted. And they will mask their personal conviction by finding something to criticize. Nine times out of ten, criticism is a defense mechanism. We criticize in others what we don't like about ourselves.

When David got home his wife gave him an earful. Michal is dripping with sarcasm: "How the King of Israel has distinguished himself today, disrobing in the sight of the slave girls."

You know what impresses me about David? It's not his kingliness. It's the fact that David wasn't afraid of taking off his royal robes. Those robes symbolized his identity and security as King of Israel. And I'm guessing there was added pressure to act like a king at the inauguration. He had a reputation to protect. He had a crown to represent. And kings don't disrobe and dance.

No one knew that better than Michal. After all, she was a "KK"—a king's kid. She grew up in the palace. She knew the protocol. And I'm guessing that her father Saul was very kingly. In fact, I think Saul woke up with scratches on his face because he slept with his crown on his head. Saul was all about image. But David was all about substance. He didn't find his identity and security in his position as King of Israel. He found his identity and security in the God who anointed him King of Israel.

So David disrobes and dances without inhibition before the Lord.

I'm sure David was frustrated. It is the greatest day of his life, and his wife takes some of the joy out of it by criticizing him. But David sticks to his guns.

"It was before the LORD, who chose me rather than your father or anyone in his house when he appointed me ruler over the LORD's people Israel—I will celebrate before the LORD. I will become even more undignified than this, and I will be humiliated in my own eyes."

Another translation says it this way:

"I am willing to act like a fool in order to show my joy in the LORD. Yes, and I am willing to look even more foolish than this."

Part of spiritual maturity is caring less and less about what people think about you and more and more about what God thinks about you. Part of taking God more seriously is taking yourself less seriously. The holiest and healthiest people in the world are those who laugh at themselves the most. And I'm guessing David and his men laughed for years about this flash dance. I seriously doubt David would have been invited to participate in *Dancing with the Stars*. I'm sure he got ribbed. I'm sure his bodyguards, including Benaiah, mimicked his dance. *Let's do the David.* But I'm guessing that no one laughed louder than David himself.

I just don't think David cared one iota about what the people in his royal entourage thought of his dancing skills. David wasn't dancing for human applause. He was dancing before God. And I'm guessing God Himself got a good laugh that day.

One Hebrew word for worship is *hallal.* It means "clamorously foolish."

In a sense, worship is foolish, isn't it? Singing to someone you can't see. Raising your hands to someone you can't touch.

Every once in a while, if the right song comes on the radio, Lora and I throw a little impromptu dance party in our Dodge Caravan. We'll turn up the volume and bust out some moves. Our heads are banging and our bodies are swaying. And if we really get into it, our minivan is rocking back and forth. Our kids think we're crazy—but the person in the car behind us thinks we are *really* crazy.

But who is crazy? Is it us? Or is it the people who can't hear the music? I'd like to think the crazy people are the ones who aren't dancing because they can't hear the music.

There is an old proverb: "Those who hear not the music think the dancer is mad."

That's what is happening in 2 Samuel 6, isn't it? David hears the music. Michal doesn't.

So who's crazy?

All I know is this: If we had ultrasonic hearing that allowed us to tune in to heaven's frequency and hear angels singing, the music would literally lift us off our feet. I'm guessing we'd dance like David danced.

I think David gives us a picture of pure worship. Worship is disrobing. It is taking off those things outside our relationship with Christ that we find our identity and security in. It is a reminder that our royal robes are like "filthy rags." It's not about what we can do for God. It's about what God has done for us. And that understanding produces the greatest freedom in the world: having nothing to prove. Instead of trying to prove himself as the King of Israel, David was consumed with worshiping the King of Kings.

Uncivilized

There is a powerful scene in *Rocky III*. Of course, all the scenes in all the *Rocky* movies are powerful, aren't they?

For what it's worth, if *In a Pit with a Lion on a Snowy Day* is ever made into a movie, I know who I'd want to cast as Benaiah. I think Benaiah was part Rocky and part Rambo. But if I couldn't get Sylvester Stallone, I guess I'd settle for Mel Gibson or Russell Crowe. Benaiah seems like a mixture of William Wallace and Maximus.

I love the scene where Rocky is getting soft. He is getting cultured. He has achieved boxing fame, and he loses his fighting fire. And his manager, Mickey, says to Rocky, "The worst thing happened that could happen to any fighter—you got civilized."

I wonder if that is exactly what Jesus would say to us.

You got civilized.

When I read the Gospels, the only civilized people I see are the Pharisees. John the Baptist was uncivilized. Just look at his diet and dress. He ate locusts and wore camel hair. It sure seems like Jesus handpicked a dozen disciples who were totally undomesticated. And Jesus himself was untamed.

In the words of Dorothy Sayers:

> The people who hanged Christ never, to do them justice, accused Him of being a bore—on the contrary; they thought Him too dynamic to be safe. It has been left for

later generations to muffle up that shattering personality and surround Him with an atmosphere of tedium. We have very efficiently pared the claws of the Lion of Judah, certified Him "meek and mild," and recommended Him as a fitting household pet for pale curates and pious old ladies.[7]

One of my favorite gospel episodes is when Jesus threw down with the moneychangers. He turned a routine Passover into a circus act or riot act.

Jesus made a whip from some ropes and chased them all out of the Temple. He drove out the sheep and oxen, scattered the money changers' coins over the floor, and turned over tables.

To be perfectly honest, this temple tantrum used to cause internal dissonance. It didn't fit my flannelgraph caricature of who Jesus was. It seemed out of character. But I think we underestimate and underappreciate this side of Jesus. We tend to picture Jesus only as the meek Lamb of God. But on that day, there was holy fire in his eyes.

And the coolest part of the story to me is that Jesus made the whip himself. Jump back Indiana Jones!

I'm impressed with guys who can change their own oil, but this takes machismo to a whole new level. I think the disciples' jaws were sore the next day because they dropped so hard when they saw Jesus flex his righteous muscles. This incident revealed a dimension of Jesus' personality that they hadn't noticed before: "Then his disciples remembered this prophecy from the Scriptures, 'Passion for God's house burns within me.'"

I have a core conviction: Christ followers ought to be the most passionate people on the planet. To be like Jesus is to be consumed with passion. The word *enthusiasm* comes from two Greek words, *en* and *Theos*, which together mean *in God*. The more we get into God, the more passionate we become.

Lion chasers aren't afraid of conflict. They aren't afraid of risking their reputation by chasing snakes out of the temple. And they aren't afraid of risking their lives chasing a lion into a pit. They often look foolish while *in the act*. It almost seems like they have a death wish. But lion chasers have a *life wish*. They live life to the fullest because they are willing to look foolish.

CHAPTER 8 REVIEW

Points to Remember

- You have to be willing to look foolish in the world's eyes.
- If you aren't willing to look foolish, you're foolish. In fact, faith requires a willingness to look foolish.
- Maturity doesn't equal conformity.
- The way we grow up spiritually is by becoming more and more like little children.
- Self-consciousness isn't just a curse. It's part of The Curse.
- Part of spiritual maturity is caring less and less about what people think of you and more and more about what God thinks of you.
- Christ followers ought to be the most passionate people on the planet. To be like Jesus is to be consumed with passion.

Starting Your Chase

Mark says that "lion chasers live life to the fullest because they are willing to look foolish." Do you feel like you're missing out on blessings because you're too afraid of looking like a fool? Try doing one important "foolish" thing for God today and see if the blessing isn't greater than the embarrassment.

CHAPTER 9

Unleash the Lion Chaser Within

Fear not that thy life shall come to an end,
but rather fear that it shall never have a beginning.

JOHN CARDINAL NEWMAN

When I was in seminary, I felt like God gave me two dreams to pursue. One dream was planting a church. The other dream was writing a book. I had no idea how or when either of those dreams would become reality, but I knew they were lions I was called to chase.

I've been living the church dream for the past decade serving as lead pastor of National Community Church in Washington DC. But chasing the writing dream was a much more precipitous and circuitous path. I started pastoring National Community Church shortly after seminary, but the writing dream was full of missteps and false starts. I have half a dozen half-finished manuscripts saved on my hard drive and a few rejection letters saved in my files. So while I feel as called to write as I do to pastor, there were moments over the last ten years when I wished that God hadn't even downloaded the writing dream. It was like a pebble in my shoe, a constant source of irritation and frustration. The longer I went without fulfilling that dream, the longer the shadow it cast on the rest of my life.

Then, a few years ago, I self-published my first book. I wish I could tell you that it was a *New York Times* bestseller. It wasn't. In fact, it only sold fifty-seven copies its first month in print. My first royalty check was a whopping $110.43. Let's just say that Lora and I didn't start making early retirement plans. But I kept chasing the lion.

After nearly a decade of dream frustration, supernatural synchronicities started happening right and left. In chapter 1 I referenced one of my core convictions: God is in the business of strategically positioning us in the right place at the right time. That isn't just good theory. It is reality. I have an unshakable sense of destiny because I know that as long as I pursue God's calling on my life, then God is ultimately responsible for getting me where He wants me to go. The same goes for you. And I hope and pray that *In a Pit with a Lion on a Snowy Day* is one of those supernatural synchronicities that helps you chase your lions.

LION CHASING SKILLS

We've talked about seven different skills you'll need if you want to be a lion chaser. You have to start by trying to comprehend the infiniteness of God so that you can believe He can help you to defy the odds. You have to face your fears, or they'll hold you back forever. You have to learn to reframe your problems through Scripture reading, prayer, and worship. Then you'll shift your perspective so that your problem becomes less significant and God's greatness becomes more evident.

And remember, you *must* take risks. That is the essence of faith. Then you're ready to seize the opportunity. But you have to be able to see it to seize it. That means getting yourself in tune with the Holy Spirit. You have to listen to His still, small voice prompting you and

IN A PIT WITH A LION ON A SNOWY DAY 169

believe that He is setting you up for success. And finally, you have to accept that you're going to look foolish sometimes. Chasing a lion usually looks pretty crazy to everyone else. But following Christ is doing the will of God no matter how foolish you might look in the process.

These skills are a package deal. You can't just pick and choose one or two of them. It is all or nothing. And if you apply all of them, you'll start living life to the fullest.

So let me ask you: *What lion is God calling you to chase?*

Lock eyes with the lion. Why would God be putting it in front of you? What good thing might God have waiting for you on the other side of this challenge? Maybe there's a lesson He wants you to learn or a blessing He wants to give you. Don't just focus on the fear factor. Try to see the bigger picture.

What will you miss out on if you let your fears dictate your choices? Is being "safe" really worth it? Maybe God wants to show you something about yourself or Himself, but you'll never know what it is unless you chase your lion. And once you have the lion cornered in the pit, you'll discover that his roar is worse than his bite when you've got God on your side.

So what's your first move? What can you do today to get a little closer to catching that lion? Your first step may be small, but that doesn't make it inconsequential. As long as you're following in the footsteps of Christ, each small step will be a giant leap.

I'm convinced that many of us are one lion chase away from our dreams becoming reality. I can't promise it will be a short chase or an easy chase. It will involve fear and uncertainty and risk. But where you end up in life really comes down to how you react when you cross paths with a lion.

If you run away from the lion, you'll one day realize that you're really running away from yourself—and God. Your problems and dreams will continue to haunt you. But the good news is that you can always turn around, and God will give you a second chance.

When I read a good book, the Holy Spirit has a way of surfacing thoughts and feelings that have lain dormant for months or years. Sometimes a forgotten dream resurfaces. Or an unresolved problem. Or an unnoticed opportunity.

As you've read *In a Pit with a Lion on a Snowy Day*, I hope the Holy Spirit has surfaced things in your spirit: problems that need to be reframed, risks that need to be taken, fears that need to be unlearned.

I hope this book gives you the courage to chase the lions in your life.

THE CHASING GENE

One of my favorite DC destinations is Roosevelt Island. It sits in the middle of the Potomac River near Georgetown. My kids love the island because it is a natural habitat in the middle of an urban jungle. Plus, you have to cross a foot bridge to get there. They love chasing lizards and catching tadpoles, but our last trip involved an unforgettable encounter with larger game. We were looking for lizards when Parker spotted a herd of whitetail deer less than ten feet off the footpath.

I had no idea there were deer on the island. And I have no idea how they got there. But we spent the next half hour chasing deer through the underbrush and Parker, Summer, and Josiah were in the zone. They had the time of their lives! Why? Because kids love chasing things. Especially wild things.

My kids love chasing butterflies. They love chasing rabbits. They love chasing their dad. And they love chasing each other.

It's almost like we are born with a *chasing gene*. It's part of our

DNA. We need something to chase. We may grow up and stop chasing butterflies, but we still need something to chase. So guys chase girls and girls chase guys. We chase academic or athletic or artistic goals. We chase degrees. We chase positions.

I believe that God created us to chase lions, but too often that chase ends in miscarriage or misdirection. We stop chasing. Or we chase the wrong things that lead us down the wrong path.

Maybe it is time to start chasing God again. Maybe it is time to seize God-ordained opportunities. Maybe it is time unleash the lion chaser within.

Chase the lion!

It's what you are destined to do.

Acknowledgments

Without the support and encouragement of my wife, Lora, this book would have never seen the light of day. I love chasing lions with you!

Without parents who believed in me more than I believed in myself, I'm not sure I would have had the courage to chase lions.

Thanks to my church family, National Community Church in Washington DC. I wouldn't want to be anyplace else doing anything else with anyone else. Thanks for the privilege of serving you.

To our staff, I love doing life and ministry with you. Thanks for what you do and who you are!

To Brian McLaren, thanks for your encouragement as I began this writing journey.

To John Eames, thanks for partnering with me in this calling.

To the Multnomah team, I never imagined that partnering with a publisher would be this enjoyable. Thanks for your tireless effort in turning this dream into reality.

To Kevin Marks, thanks for inviting me to join the team and your timely encouragement along the way. To my editors, David Kopp and Adrienne Spain, thanks for your wisdom and patience and courage. You made me a better writer. To Jason Myhre, thanks for infusing your creativity into this project. To Jake Burts, thanks for keeping us on task and on time.

Endnotes

SCRIPTURE

Chapter 1: Locking Eyes with Your Lion

There was also Benaiah son of Jehoiada…—2 Samuel
23:20–21, NLT

Chapter 2: The Odd Thing About Odds

The description of the Egyptian is found in 1 Chronicles 11:23.
"You have too many men…"—Judges 7:2
"There are still too many men."—Judges 7:4
"You have too many warriors…"— Judges 7:2, NLT
Now the earth was formless and empty…— Genesis 1:2
I look behind me and you're there…— Psalm 139:5
…a day is like a thousand years…—2 Peter 3:8
"My thoughts are not your thoughts…"— Isaiah 55:8
The verse that states God thought of planned for everything we
     need is Ephesians 1:11
We are God's workmanship…—Ephesians 2:10
"Alas, master! For it was borrowed." —2 Kings 6:5, NKJV
And the iron did swim. —2 Kings 6:6, KJV
"Eight months' wages would not buy enough…"—John 6:7
Jesus then took the loaves…—John 6:11–13
The story and meaning of Ebenezer is found in 1 Samuel 7:6–12,
     KJV.

Whatever you bind on earth will be bound in heaven...—Matthew
    18:18

The "scroll of remembrance" is mentioned in Malachi 3:16.

The phrase "apple of his eye" is used in Zechariah 2:8.

Chapter 3: Unlearning Your Fears

"You have heard that it was said, 'Eye for an eye'..."—Matthew
    5:38–39

"You have heard that it was said, 'Do not commit adultery.'..."—
    Matthew 5:27–28

"You have heard that it was said, 'Love your neighbor'..."—
    Matthew 5:43–44

"I have no one to help me into the pool..."—John 5:7

"Stand up, pick up your sleeping mat, and walk!"—John 5:8, NLT

Do not conform any longer...—Romans 12:2

Let this mind be in you...—Philippians 2:5, NKJV

Let the word of Christ dwell in you richly. — Colossians 3:16

Your enemy the devil prowls...— I Peter 5:8

Satan is referred to as "the accuser of our brethren" in Revelation
    12:10.

John 18:4 (NLT) says that Jesus stepped forward when his enemies
    came to arrest him.

He was led like a sheep to the slaughter...—Acts 8:32

"If you are the King of the Jews, save yourself." —Luke 23:37

"Do you think I cannot call on my Father..."—Matthew 26:53–54

Shadrach, Meshach and Abednego replied to the king...—Daniel
    3:16–18

King Nebuchadnezzar leaped to his feet...—Daniel 3:24–25

Nebuchadnezzar said, "Praise be to the God..."—Daniel 3:28

Chapter 4: The Art of Reframing

David is named as the captain of King Saul's bodyguard in I Samuel
    22:14.

When a lion or a bear came...—I Samuel 17:34

A mob quickly formed against Paul and Silas...—Acts 16:22–24,
    NLT

Around midnight, Paul and Silas were praying...—Acts 16:25, NLT

Suddenly there was such a violent earthquake...—Acts 16:26

God comforts us in all our troubles...—2 Corinthians 1:4

It has been granted to you on behalf of Christ...—Philippians 1:29

Five times I received from the Jews...—2 Corinthians 11:24–27

Chapter 5: Guaranteed Uncertainty

Perhaps the LORD will act in our behalf.—I Samuel 14:6

He went without knowing where he was going.—Hebrews 11:8, NLT

Noah did everything exactly as God had commanded him.—Genesis
    6:22, NLT

When the day of Pentecost came...—Acts 2:1–4

The parable of the talents is found in Matthew 25:14–30.

"Foxes have holes and birds of the air have nests..."—Matthew
    8:20

...a peace that passes understanding...—Philippians 4:7

The story of Jesus turning water into wine at the wedding in Cana is
    found in John 2:1–11.

The story of Joseph is found in Genesis 37–50.

Give ear to my words...—Psalm 5:1

The Holy Spirit helps us in our distress...—Romans 8:26

Chapter 6: Playing It Safe Is Risky

...more honored than the other members of the Thirty...—Samuel 23:23, NLT

If I perish, I perish. —Esther 4:16

If it pleases the king...—Nehemiah 2:5

We do not need to defend ourselves...—Daniel 3:16–17

We cannot help speaking...—Acts 4:20

The parable of the talents is found in Matthew 25:14–30.

Some faced jeers and flogging...—Hebrews 11:36–38

"If anyone would come after me, he must deny himself and take up his cross and follow me. For whoever wants to save his life will lose it, but whoever loses his life for me will find it."—Matthew 16:24–25

"I tell you the truth, at the renewal of all things..."—Matthew 19:28–29

"Don't be afraid."... "Lord, it it's you..." "Come."—Matthew 14:27–29

When [Peter] saw the wind...—Matthew 14:30

"From the days of John the Baptist until now..."—Matthew 11:12

Chapter 7: Grab Opportunity by the Mane

Scripture says Benaiah was commander of twenty-four thousand men in I Chronicles 27:5.

Do not despise these small beginnings...—Zechariah 4:10, NLT

After Ehud came Shamgar...—Judges 3:31

Make the most of every opportunity...—Colossians 4:5

Devote yourselves to prayer...—Colossians 4:2

Whoever watches the wind will not plant...—Ecclesiastes 11:4

"My time has not yet come."—John 2:4

Sow your seed in the morning...—Ecclesiastes 11:6

Chapter 8: The Importance of Looking Foolish

The story of Noah is found in Genesis 5:32–9:29.

The story of Sarah is found in Genesis 11:29–23:1.

The story of the wall of Jericho is found in Joshua 5:13–6:27.

The story of David and Goliath is found in I Samuel 17:1–50.

The story of the wise men is found in Matthew 2:1–12.

The story of Peter walking on water is found in Matthew
     14:22–33.

The story of Jesus' crucifixion and resurrection is found in Matthew
     27–28, Mark 15–16, Luke 22–24, John 19–20.

God tells Ezekial to cook dung in Ezekial 4:12.

A donkey speaks in Numbers 22:28.

God tells Hosea to marry a prostitute in Hosea 1:3.

"...proclaim that captives will be released..." —Luke 4:18, NLT

"I tell you the truth, unless you change..."—Matthew 18:3

"Whoever humbles himself like this child..."—Matthew 18:4

At that moment, their eyes were opened...—Genesis 3:7, NLT

Don't be drunk with wine...—Ephesians 5:18, NLT

But as the Ark of the LORD entered the City of David...—2 Samuel
     6:16, NLT

"How the King of Israel has distinguished..."—2 Samuel 6:20

"It was before the LORD, who chose me..."—2 Samuel 6:21–22

"I am willing to act like a fool..."—2 Samuel 6:21–22, NLT

Our righteous deeds are called "filthy rags" in Isaiah 64:6.

Jesus made a whip from some ropes...—John 2:15, NLT

Then his disciples remembered this prophecy...—John 2:17

WORKS CITED

Chapter 1: Locking Eyes with Your Lion

1.   Dr. Neal Roese, *If Only: How to Turn Regret into Opportunity* (New York: Broadway, 2005), 47–48.

Chapter 2: The Odd Thing About Odds

2.   A.W. Tozer, *The Knowledge of the Holy* (San Francisco: HarperSanFrancisco, 1978), I.
3.   Ibid., VII.

Chapter 4: The Art of Reframing

1.   Viktor E. Frankl, *Man's Search for Meaning* (Boston: Beacon Press, 2006), 86.
2.   Dr. Neal Roese, *If Only: How to Turn Regret into Opportunity* (New York: Broadway, 2005), 18–19.
3.   Walter Kaufman, *Faith of a Heretic* (New York: Doubleday, 2000).

Chapter 5: Guaranteed Uncertainty

1.   Robert Fulghum, *From Beginning to End*, (New York: Ivy Books, 1996), 154.
2.   Dr. Martin Seligman, *Learned Optimism*, (New York: Free Press, 1998), 15.
3.   Ibid., 16.
4.   Ted Loder, *Guerillas of Grace: Prayers for the Battle*, (Philadelphia: Innisfree Press, 1984), 69.

Chapter 6: Playing It Safe Is Risky

1. James Gleick, *Chaos: Making a New Science*, (New York: Penguin, 1988).
2. Dr. Neal Roese, *If Only: How to Turn Regret into Opportunity* (New York: Broadway, 2005), 48.
3. Annie Dillard, *Teaching a Stone to Talk: Expeditions and Encounters*, (New York: Harper Perennial, 1988), 52–53.
4. Robert Briner, *Roaring Lambs*, (Nashville: Zondervan, 2000), 5.

Chapter 7: Grab Opportunity by the Mane

1. Howard Schultz, *Pour Your Heart into It: How Starbucks Built a Company One Cup at a Time*, (New York: Hyperion, 1999), 91.
2. Ibid., 63.
3. Ibid., 185.
4. Mark Burnett, *Jump In!: Even If You Don't Know How To Swim*, (New York: Ballantine Books, 2005), 12.

Chapter 8: The Importance of Looking Foolish

1. John Putzier, *Get Weird!: 101 Innovative Ways to Make Your Company a Great Place to Work*, (New York: American Management Association, 2001), 7–8.
2. Gordon Mackenzie, *Orbiting the Giant Hairball: A Corporate Fool's Guide to Surviving with Grace*, (New York: Viking Adult, 1998), 20.
3. Ibid., 23.
4. Ibid., 23–24.
5. Warren G. Bennis and Robert J. Thomas, *Geeks and Geezers* (Cambridge, MA: Harvard Business School Press, 2002), 20.
6. Ronald Rolheiser, *Against an Infinite Horizon: The Finger of God in Our Everyday Lives* (New York: Crossroad, 2002).

7. Dorothy Sayers, "The Greatest Drama Ever Staged," *Letters to a Diminished Church*, (Nashville: W Publishing Group, 2004).

Most of us have no idea where we're going most of the time.

MARK BATTERSON
AUTHOR OF *In A Pit with a Lion on a Snowy Day*

WILD GOOSE CHASE

Reclaim the Adventure of Pursuing God

Most of us have no idea where we are going most of the time. And I know that is unsettling. But circumstantial uncertainty also goes by another name: "Adventure."

Celtic Christians had a name for the Holy Spirit—*An Geadh-Glas,* or 'the Wild Goose.' The name hints at mystery. Much like a wild goose, the Spirit of God cannot be tracked or tamed. An element of danger, an air of unpredictability surround Him. And while the name may sound a little sacrilegious, I cannot think of a better description of what it's like to follow the Spirit through life. I think the Celtic Christians were on to something....

—Mark Batterson, *Wild Goose Chase*

Resources available online at chasethegoose.com.

MULTNOMAH BOOKS
www.waterbrookmultnomah.com

Be Astonished Again

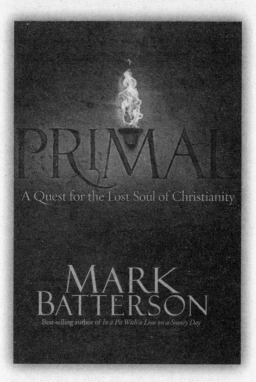

What would your Christianity look like if it was stripped down to the simplest, rawest, purest faith possible? You would have more, not less. You would have the beginning of a new reformation—in your generation, your church, your own soul. You would have *primal* Christianity.

This book is an invitation to become part of a reformation movement. It is an invitation to rediscover the compassion, wonder, curiosity, and energy that turned the world upside down two thousand years ago. It is an invitation to be astonished again.

 MULTNOMAH BOOKS
www.waterbrookmultnomah.com